The Couple's Journey

Intimacy as a Path to Wholeness

Susan M. Campbell, Ph.D.

Impact 🕮 Publishers
POST OFFICE BOX 1094
SAN LUIS OBISPO, CALIFORNIA 93406

Library of Congress Cataloging in Publication Data

Campbell, Susan M   1941-
    The couple's journey.

    1. Marriage. 2. Interpersonal relations.
3. Intimacy (Psychology) 4. Sex in marriage.
5. Maturation (Psychology) I. Title.
HQ734.C263   301.42   79-23836
ISBN 0-915166-45-3

PUBLISHER'S NOTE

Cover design by Gordon Hayduk.
Typesetting by Dexter & Magee, San Luis Obispo, California.
Printed in the United States of America.

Published by

Impact *Publishers*
POST OFFICE BOX 1094
SAN LUIS OBISPO, CALIFORNIA 93406

CONTENTS

SECTION II — FOR PROFESSIONAL COUNSELORS

INTRODUCTION

Intimacy as a Path to Wholeness

This book is a roadmap. It is a roadmap for a particular kind of journey — the journey of two people toward intimacy. Like all maps, it won't *take* you to your destination, but will tell you something of what you may expect along the way.

I've prepared this map to assist couples and would-be couples to find their way along that path, and hopefully to discover new meaning and purpose in the couple relationship.

While the pairing instinct has always been a major force in personal and social evolution, the current incredible pace of social and global change results in a subtle but deeply felt "meaning crisis" for many. As individual persons become increasingly aware that they have a *choice* to pair or not, as well as to parent or not, questions of *meaning* and choice come more and more into the foreground:

Why are we doing this?

What does it mean that we've chosen each other?

What difference does it make whether or not we stay together?

In my extensive counseling work with couples over the past 12

1

years, I have witnessed and guided many intimate journeys. And although every couple is unique, all seemed to have at least one thing in common — the search for a sense of meaning:

A sense that their daily individual struggles made sense in some kind of social or global *context*.

A sense that they could *learn* and *grow* from their experiences rather than repeating the same trials and errors over and over and over.

A sense that they could have an *impact* on their surroundings — on the culture as well as on their partner.

A sense that their life made a *difference,* no matter how small, in the overall scheme of things.

Obstacles and Illusions

In guiding couples toward actualizing their inner sense of wholeness, I have been conscious of the tremendous obstacles that people must overcome in the quest — obstacles that seem almost to be "deliberately" placed in their path by Life in order to test the wit and merit of the seeker. In our Western culture such obstacles tend to occur somewhat predictably. They can be seen as illusions stemming from how our personalities develop and how we are socialized — illusions which, when clung to, lead the journeyors into one cul-de-sac after another.

Both my couples counseling work and my research into the area of relationships have revealed to me time and again how perfectly suited is the man-woman relationship to teaching us about the nature of such illusions. It offers an ideal context for seeing the obstacles to true relationship in oneself and in the culture; and it provides, as well, a unique opportunity for overcoming the illusions which create these obstacles.

In my counseling work with individuals and couples, I have been struck by how many people come to me with one of the following complaints: if they are not currently involved in a pair relationship, "Why can't I find someone to be with? Is there something lacking in me, perhaps?" And if they *are* currently coupled: "My partner and I are having problems getting along; how can we have a more satisfying relationship?" Thus, the vast majority of my clientele I find to be either unhappy in-love or unhappy out-of-love. Their problems seem to be in relation to relationships.

This is not only true of people who seek the assistance of a counselor. My friends and colleagues and most everyone I meet seem also to be dealing with these issues in one way or another. And I have experienced in my own relationships almost all of the problems described in this book.

Through my experiences as a counselor, friend, lover, wife, and researcher, I have become convinced that if we can better *understand* the process of creating an intimate relationship, we will be more able to find satisfaction in the process.

When we realize, for example, that "it's supposed to hurt sometimes," that it's not always a bed of roses, then we can respond creatively to the situation, rather than attempting to avoid it.

When we recognize the importance of the "changes" we're going through, we can respond with more presence of mind and less fear. Just as the pain of childbirth has become "meaningful pain" due to mass prenatal education, I hope now to help couples see the meaning in the inevitable changes that they encounter on their journeys toward intimacy.

There seems a somewhat predictable pattern of obstacles to relationship: a pattern which, for each of us, stems from the structure of our personalities and from how we are socialized. These obstacles often take the form of illusions about ourselves which we must peel away, layer after layer, if we are to realize our deepest selves. And just as the layers of an onion have different qualities, depending on how close we are to its center, so too do the stages of development in the couples journey. Each stage contains obstacles and/or illusions to be peeled away, and some learnings which occur as a result. As the work of each stage is completed or realized, a new developmental task emerges with its own illusions to be overcome.

The journey toward wholeness, toward true relationship, is a never-ending process. We are continually letting go of the old and embracing the new, continually expanding the boundaries of our very selves.

While the journey itself has a landscape unique to each couple, there do seem to be certain recurring obstacles and learnings which nearly everyone will encounter on the path. Thus a map can be constructed for the journey, showing the usual order of events, and what the terrain looks like at each point. The chapters which follow will develop the details of the map, so that you may locate yourself on the path, get a better perspective on where you've been, where you are now, and what likely lies ahead.

The map I have prepared describes the five key stages of the Journey: from *Romance* to *Power Struggle* to *Stability* to *Commitment* to *Co-Creation* — each stage with its own obstacles, illusions, pitfalls and potentialities.

My data for this map has grown out of three primary sources: my work as a couples' therapist with over 100 couples during the past 12 years; my own life experience; and in-depth interviews with over 50 couples engaged in becoming more conscious about their relationships.

These interviews were conducted during the past 3 years in order to check the validity of my clinical observations. This research was systematic and yet flexible, and aimed at encouraging couples to detail the historical development of their relationship as they experienced it.

Thus, in addition to information about "what happened", I was equally interested in "how it felt" to each member of the pair.

The interviews generally began with a series of introductory warm-up questions such as, "How long have you been a couple?" "How did you meet?" and "Do you recall what first attracted you to each other?"

The key question asked of all the couples interviewed was: "Most couples find that their relationship goes through various changes over the years. Could you reflect back on your relationship, from the beginning up to now, and describe how it has evolved and changed? Perhaps there've been some major turning points or events that have marked or sparked these changes. Just go back in time to how it was 10 years ago (for example) and I'll ask questions to help keep us focused."

All interviews were conducted by me in the couples' homes. Each interview required 2-3 hours' time. All interviews were tape recorded with the couples' permission.

My interviewees were all heterosexual couples from middle class backgrounds. They were widely situated geographically (from New York to California) and ranged in length of time together from 3 years to 30 years. About two-thirds were married, while one-third were unmarried but living together.

They had been referred to me by friends and colleagues as people engaged in developing greater awareness or consciousness about their relationships. I chose to talk with this select group of couples because I felt they had something to teach me.

Thus the experiences of these couples have provided the material for my description of the mythic journey of the modern couple, presented here in terms of a developmental sequence of events, illustrated by case material, vignettes, and poetry.

The aim of this book is to help you:

1. to determine how you got to where you are in the developmental process and to see where it is that you now may wish to go in order to make your lives more fulfilling.
2. to find meaning in the often confusing process of living intimately with another person by seeing how others have used their struggles to foster deeper self-understanding.
3. to re-vision coupling as a vehicle for attaining psychological and spiritual harmony or wholeness for the couple, and ultimately for everyone you touch.
4. (most importantly) to understand and accept that coupling, like life, is a continually changing process. There are (almost) *no insurmountable problems*, since if we stay with a situation long enough it will change into something else (or at least our perspective on it will change). Yet there are also (almost) *no lasting solutions*, since each "solution" sets the stage for the emergence of new problems.

Thus, the developmental map presented here is my way of emphasizing that there is purpose and direction to the journey; that struggle is a necessary part of it; and that it can be most rich and alive if we pay attention to all of our experiences along the way.

The *vehicle* for the journey is the developing couple relationship. The *destination* (never quite fully attained) is wholeness: that ideal state in which all my parts are in harmonious communication with each other, with my partner and with the world beyond our partnership. It is that state when "everything's working together."

Viewing the development of an intimate pair relationship as a spiritual journey emphasizes the inseparability of self-actualization and relationship-actualization. The self is felt to be meaningful only when one is part of a larger context, i.e. in relationship with something outside or beyond oneself and thus able to stand outside oneself.

This viewpoint also emphasizes how two individuals can struggle and learn to develop their individual selves while at the same time overcoming their separateness — the two processes being essentially inseparable when seen over time.

SO-SOCIALIZATION

The couples journey
is fraught with trials
There are scores of his 'n hurdles
to be surmounted along the path

The demons devils and
vampires of excessive
thought emotion and desire
will suck our energy
if we pay attention to them

They will attempt to live through us
feeding off our unfocused energy
keeping us lusting after explanations
popularity, possessions
preventing us from trusting
our inner voice our center our Being

The world of maya
of illusion
of apparent reality
has done and will continue to do
everything in its power
to take us on its trip
rather than our own

We've been so-socialized
and hypnotized
that we have very little idea
who we really are

We learn to seek
but never to find
to want
but never to have
to achieve
but never to receive

to work harder and harder
to justify our existence
in a world we never wanted
to be in

The illusion of duality
is essential to the
maintenance of our
materialistic chauvinistic hedonistic
society
and to all the "fun"
we had being teenagers —
learning that boys like sex
and girls don't

And how if you're a boy
your goal is to "score"
and if you're a girl
your concern is to
keep him from scoring
(or at least to keep the score down)

And we learned how
to be big boys and not to cry
and to be good girls and never hurt
other people's feelings
to be men of the world
and women of innocence
leading up to our modern-day
socially-sanctioned symptomatology
of the "rigid male"
and the "hysterical female"

Society tempts us with
empty rewards
like importance fame and glory
teases us with
seductive titillations
like excitement stimulation and pleasure

and threatens us with
boredom and isolation if we don't
take the bait

Keeping balanced
between the scylla of overstimulation
and the charybdis of deprivation
is a challenge
for any couple

And besides the outer-worldly pressures
we have the noisy cast of characters
in our inner drama
to contend with:
the greedy one who wants it all
on a silver platter
the pretty one who tries to steal
every show
or the professor who relates only
through the lessons he's teaching
or the guru whose holy attitude
is surpassed only by his self-righteousness

We've been taught
that these roles
are necessary
if we want
to be somebody

and besides what else is there to do?

We could try relating sexually
but we learned long ago
that anything as potentially pleasurable
as sex
must be bad
so we can't really enjoy it fully

which keeps us stuck at this level —
seeking but never quite finding

fully satisfying sexual relationships

*which keeps us from moving on
to more refined and spiritual
ways of using our sexual energy*

*which leads to the "repression of the sublime"
in man-woman
to our being totally out of touch
with the loving creative altruistic
aspects of our unconscious
and to our identifying with the
Freudian notion of our
underlying selfish destructive and sadistic
potentials*

*We've been so-socialized
to believe in darkness
rather than light
in scarcity
rather than abundance
in seeing parts
rather than wholes
that we find ourselves
hesitating unhesitatingly
economizing extravagantly
and discriminating indiscriminately*

*If we buy into
these definitions of man-woman
we find ourselves shrinking
our world to fit them*

*Let's not forget that
the way we define ourselves
is the way we find ourselves
the couples journey being
a way to re-de-find ourselves*

Thus, the aim of the Couple's Journey is to experience a quality of relationship where my love for myself and my love for my partner are two inseparable parts of a whole — where getting what I want serves *us*, and giving to *you* serves *me* as well. This inseparability of self and other is what the term "wholeness" implies: We recognize our unity, even while celebrating our uniqueness.

Overview

I have organized the first part of the book around a description of the process of developing an intimate relationship:

Chapters One through Five offer detailed descriptions, case histories, and personal anecdotes on each of the five major developmental stages of the Couple's Journey: Romance, Power, Stability, Commitment, Co-Creation.

Chapter Six, "Current Issues in the Couple Relationship", extends the developmental model into areas beyond the scope of my research, dealing with some important issues which are touched on in earlier chapters, but which deserve further discussion and study: sexual exclusivity (i.e. monogamy - nonmonogamy); sex roles, sex and lovemaking; spiritual practice; and individual differences.

Chapter Seven summarizes the key issues and learnings of the Couple's Journey, while Chapter Eight offers a collection of self-help activities which couples can use at various stages on the path.

Chapters Nine and Ten make up the section for professional counselors. Chapter Nine, "The Couples Therapist as Guide," looks at how couples can use a counselor to facilitate their journey toward wholeness. Chapter Ten, "The Couples Group Intensive," describes a process for fostering mutual support among couples on similar journeys as a way to strengthen their commitment to conscious personal and social transformation.

Let's look briefly at the stages on the Couple's Journey.

The Five Stages of the Couple's Journey

I. Romance: Here the couple is inspired by their vision of "how it's supposed to be:" by the promise that this person has some special something that one has longed for. There is the illusion of unity; fantasies of a harmonious future; a diffuse and undifferentiated sense of "we-ness". Partners deny feelings of difference or separateness by creating various "dependencies" within the relationship, such as the "can't live without you" feeling. Often such feelings of "promise" stem from men's and women's stereotyped visions of an ideal mate.

The obstacle to be overcome at this point is the illusion of romance — that dreams come true for the dreaming, that wishing makes it so, that life is just a bowl of cherries, and that people naturally relate harmoniously without regard for vested interests and individual differences.

This stage comes to an end once the going gets rough and partners see that their visions and dreams are not going to be realized as easily as they had hoped. Some couples end the relationship once this begins to happen. Others face the loss of their vision by moving on to the next stage — the power struggle.

II. Power Struggle: This stage begins with the recognition that "you're not who I thought you were" or "we're not who we though we were." The illusion of unity is replaced by the disillusion of disunity. Instead of a *vision*, we experience *di-vision:* differentness, difficulty. The relationship held such promise, but the promise has been broken. We feel disillusioned, disappointed, angry.

But maybe, just maybe, we can get what we want after all if we really *try*. If we're willing to fight for it. Thus, some people's power struggle is an attempt to get the partner to be the way he or she was supposed to be, the way he or she *promised* to be (an attempt to overcome our sudden sense of powerlessness).

For others, the power struggle becomes (unconsciously) a way of hurting the partner in retaliation for the disappointment one has suffered. In this case, it takes the form of a "spite war" where each time you disappoint me, I return with a spiteful act designed to hurt you back.

The obstacle to be overcome in this stage is the illusion of power, i.e. the belief that threat, force, manipulation, or domination, no matter how subtle, can get us what we want. The stage comes to an end when we recognize who we *are* and what we *do* have, and give up our attachment to fantasies of harmony without struggle, achievement without effort, pleasure without pain. When we surrender to life as it is.

The "battle of the sexes" can dominate much of the play during this stage, with sexual differences being blamed for much of the difficulty: "If only you weren't so typically rigidly male..." "If only you weren't so typically hysterically female." Thus, the struggle continues as long as men and women continue to see another and themselves as members of stereotypical categories rather than as free and unique beings.

This stage can go on for years once the partners learn the routine — as in the case of George and Martha in Albee's play *Who's Afraid of Virginia Wolf?* It can also end abruptly if either or both see that they are going to have to confront aspects of themselves that may be too painful to face.

If the relationship survives the power struggle, it moves into a more accepting, more peaceful stage, which I've called Stability.

III. Stability: This stage begins with the experience of forgiveness. Partners give up their tenacious hold on "making it work" and allow themselves and one another their foibles and failures. They come to accept one another as individual persons and to learn from their conflicts rather than being upset by them. They may focus more of their attention outside the relationship or within their own psyches, having recognized that the pair relationship, being only one part of their lives, is not going to meet all their needs.

They have now evolved a stable set of rules for negotiating differences and a stable set of role expectations. Since these rules and patterns seem to "work", they are generally content not to question them. Often the pattern adopted parallels the culture's definition of how a "married couple" should look and behave. In other cases, great care is taken to make sure that roles are defined equally and non-stereotypically.

The obstacle to be overcome in this stage is the illusion of peace, the attachment to stability at the cost of novelty and change. When feelings of peace are so hard-won, we do not like to let go easily. And so we make a god of our new-found comfort, forgetting that growth involves risk, pain and uncertainty, all of which may be felt as we continue the journey.

IV. Commitment: In this stage the partners truly surrender to what is — and to their acceptance of the realities and human shortcomings of the relationship. They can give up trying to "remodel" the partner, and trying to be agreeable at all costs. They are able to handle the tension and conflict inherent in the problem of loving the person and hating something the person does. They can love one another without necessarily liking one another at all times.

This ability to "bind tension" to manage seemingly polarized opposites, allows them the freedom to challenge and question one another without getting into a power struggle. And it fosters in the relationship the ability to deliberately *choose* one's actions with a sense of commitment over time, since freedom is experienced in the act of choosing and is not tied to some pre-structured set of regulations guaranteeing one's autonomy.

Thus, the commitment stage is marked by the dissolution of familiar "either-or"-type categories and by the development of creative solutions to conflicts. Thinking is paradoxical rather than dichotomous, so that apparent dichotomies such as "living in the now" vs. "commitment in a future together" do not tear the couple apart or throw them into taking the "two sides" of the argument.

There is, however, one major pitfall that can occur with couples at this stage — the illusion of separateness: "we have done what's necessary to harmonize our differences as a couple...our work is complete...we need not concern ourselves with the world beyond ourselves."

Couples who continue their evolution through this stage come to understand the interconnectedness among all human beings everywhere — an interdependence which parallels that experienced by the couple.

V. Co-Creation: In this stage, the couple applies to the world beyond their partnership all they have learned during the previous four stages. They are now able to extend the feeling of human unity experienced in their relationship, and to offer to others the fruits of their mutual creativity. Thus, at this stage, couples often engage in shared creative work aimed at making a contribution in the world.

A potential pitfall of this stage is the tendency of some couples to focus so much attention on their relationship to "the world" that little energy is available for the "care and feeding" of the pair relationship itself.

Table I summarizes the major learnings and pitfalls of each stage. These will be further elaborated in the next five chapters.

TABLE I

STAGE	DEVELOPMENTAL TASK(S) OF THIS STAGE (WHAT COUPLE NEEDS TO DO OR LEARN)
I Romance	We sense our possibilities. We create a shared vision.
II Power Struggle	We learn to recognize and validate differing needs and perceptions. We learn to say who we are and ask for what we want.
III Stability	We each learn to take responsibility for our formerly unconscious (or "disowned") parts. We clarify and expand our senses of identity through dialogue with the other.
IV Commitment	We experience ourselves as an interdependent, synergistic "we-system." We learn to live with life's insoluble dilemmas and paradoxes.
V Co-Creation	We learn to cooperate with the forces that be toward creating a saner and more humane world. We become the creators of our own universe. We experience ourselves as interdependent with all of life.

PITFALLS OR ILLUSIONS COMMON TO THIS STAGE

The illusion that "wishing makes it so."
The fear that conflict will destroy our vision.

The illusion that we can change the other person to fit our image or expectations.
The need to retaliate when we don't get what we want.

The illusion that once we've learned to "take responsibility for ourselves" we no longer need to confront differences (the "illusion of peace").

The illusion of dyadic separateness: that "we've harmonized our differences as a couple and now our work is complete... we need not concern ourselves with the world beyond."

The tendency to focus too much attention on the world and too little on the "care and feeding" of our pair relationship.

A fantasy according to one dictionary definition is "supposition with no solid foundation." It's about the future. What will be. What could be. Because we don't yet know who we may be, we must discover this over time. But how would we stay together long enough to find out, without our fantasies to act as glue?

Romance creates a feeling of oneness — a feeling that we were made for each other, a feeling of perfect harmony or fit.

Illusions and Intuitions

Romantic feelings are not entirely illusory, however. Such feelings can give us a real sense of our possibilities, of how it might be if we really actualized our highest potential for loving. Often, too, romantic "fantasies" are in a sense *intuitions* about our possible future life together. Romance can create a state of heightened *vision* — a sense of our common purpose or reason for being together. Thus, romantic feelings are vital stepping stones in the couples journey. They contain an implicit map of where we wish to go together, providing direction for subsequent journeying.

In the initial phases of the Romance stage, we often share our hopes, dreams, and visions with each other. If these visions seem to be in harmony, we create a mutual vision. We thus use the relationship — and the fact that a very significant other person validates our dreams — to reinforce our life goals and our hopes of achieving them.

While romantic feelings have an important place at all stages of the couple's journey, they may become a hindrance if we get so attached to "feeling good" that we deny or supress all other feelings. It is important to stay in touch with our initial vision, as long as we do not lose touch with our ability to see clearly our day-to-day ever-changing situations. When we can use our romantic ideals and dreams as inspiration, our journey is off to a good start. If, however, we find ourselves becoming overprotective of the delicate harmony we've created, it is time to start over. One of the couples in my study, Rita and Ron, found the need for such a new beginning.

The Delicate Harmony of Rita and Ron: Rita and Ron met during their summer vacation from college on Cape Cod, where she was a waitress and he was a waiter in a small family-style restaurant. On opposite teams during a volleyball game at the beach, they had plenty of chance to observe each other's physical presence. Ron, being quite self-conscious about his short 5'2'' stature, and believing that a man should be taller than the woman he's with, was delighted to find a woman with Rita's verve and vitality who was also short. For several years he'd been wondering if he'd ever find a woman who "took up her space" personally, who was not shy and demure, and who was also short.

Rita was also attracted to Ron's size. She had dated numerous men, all much taller than she, and had grown tired of "always having to look up" to them. "It's a pain in the neck, actually", she disclosed to Ron.

Their sexual relationship, too, provided evidence for their perfect fit, and besides this, they were both majoring in biology. They began to fantasize that they were made for each other.

Rita was able to overlook the fact that Ron drank a bit more than she was comfortable with. And Ron decided he'd better not mention the fact that she often talked too loudly and excitedly for his tastes. Otherwise, things between them seemed almost too good to be true. They enjoyed the same pastimes — water sports and sun bathing. They shared similar interests — "I was amazed and thrilled to find a woman who read the newspaper every day and all day on Sunday just as I did!" She was "happy to find a man who didn't bow to social convention the way most of my previous men friends had. Ron seemed so independent."

The shared dream of Rita and Ron was based on the expectation of companionship and fun. They each wanted someone with the qualities that they themselves possessed — sexual vitality, playfulness, an interest in biology and current affairs, sociability, and a compatible body type.

Ron and Rita came to me for couples therapy during their third year of marriage. Their romance had worn thin. He was overly involved in his work and drank too much during their free time together — this was Rita's charge against Ron. She was too flirtatious with other men and was considering taking a job as a cocktail waitress, something he considered to be "beneath her" — these were Ron's complaints against Rita.

Their sex life was still satisfying to both of them — apparently the only thing they now had in common.

They seemed to be at a real love-hate stalemate. Still, they wanted to re-create that initial feeling of romance. Or at least get a glimmer of it once in a while. This was their aim in seeking counseling.

BEGINNING

Who is this man
of my absent dreams
I never dared to hope
again

I thought I was too old
to find
beyond
myself

He looked at me
and saw
and said
"I'm there too"

So we sat under a tree
and sipped rum
and ate walnuts
and let a few impatient dreams
slip through the cool calm
and we warmed and softened
and ate more walnuts.

Since they came with the image of "how it used to be" in the foreground of their consciousness, we began our work focusing on this theme: "What was there about your partner that initially attracted you? What "promise" did the relationship hold for you? What was your vision of what you two could be together?"

As we began to take another look at how they remembered their initial hopes, they became even more disheartened, since they felt so vividly the wide gap between what they had *once* felt and what they *now* felt. Their disappointment began to turn into resignation.

They were more willing to focus on their resignation than their vision because they had seen that the vision was not so easily actualized as they had hoped it might be. It was their *illusion* about "having it on a silver platter" that needed to be discarded, not their *vision* of what was possible for them. Unfortunately, once they realized that disciplined effort and creativity would be required of them both, in order to actualize their vision, they lost sight of the vision and withdrew into working, drinking, and flirting. In a sense this resignation was helping them avoid responsibility for turning their dream into reality.

They came to me with a broken dream, like a child comes crying to a parent with a broken toy. My task was to help them *re-experience* — not just recall — their vision. They had conceived the vision together, yet it had remained dormant in the distance between them for almost 3 years. If they could experience the shared pleasure of having all their attention concentrated on one thing — *their relationship* — rather than on avoiding their anxiety about the future, perhaps they could re-kindle the feeling of aliveness.

In their state of mind at that point, there was no use trying to get them back into their romantic feelings right away. I decided to let them continue with the "blaming game" they had already begun, but this time with consciousness and full attention to what they were doing. I asked them to take turns rather than both speaking at once. In turn, first Rita and then Ron took the floor and let fly with the "If only you woulds...", the "you nevers" and "you alwayses," while the partner was instructed only to listen. They found this sort of ventilation to be at first quite embarrassing — since each had to take full responsibility for his or her own accusations and couldn't hide behind the pretense of self-defense.

After a short time, they both felt exhilarated—at last having had the chance to fully *spend* their anger. At the close of the exercise,

they felt an excitement and closeness they hadn't shared since the
early weeks of their relationship." What's going on?" they
wondered. "We thought such all-out dumping on each other would
drive us further apart. Instead we feel kind of giddy and more
alive!" I saw no need to explain, allowing them to puzzle it out on
their own during the week until our next session. At the next
session they came in more hopeful than they had felt for a long
time, yet seeing the tremendous care required to maintain an
intimate relationship. They realized that both of them had been
trying to "hang on" to the good feelings of the "honeymoon
period," at first by denying any negative feelings toward the other,
and later, when such feelings were unavoidable, by denying that
these feelings had a right to exist in an intimate relationship.

Our little "blow-out session," or "Vesuvius" as couples
therapist George Bach calls it, had shown them that *contact* is what
is satisfying between two people — not agreement at all costs. To
be in *contact*, both must be willing to experience and express what
is felt, to risk sharing the "bad" along with the good. Genuine
contact requires *concentrated* attention to what is happening in the
relationship at that moment.

Thus, as Rita and Ron overcame their prejudice against so-called
"negative" feelings, they began to feel the excitement revived in
their relationship; they were motivated to work toward creating the
shared vision of companionship that they had almost lost.

Our work was focused not so much on the *content* of their
romantic ideal, but rather on the faulty belief that it should come to
them automatically, without some pain and effort — some trial and
error — and the willingness always to begin again.

They learned, in the process of our work, that by working
together on a shared problem they were actually creating *within*
their relationship some new capacities for resolving differences.
Before doing this work together, they had been operating under the
fantasy that something *outside* their relationship would bring the
answer. They tried booze, flirting, overwork, and finally therapy —
all "outside" solutions, in a sense. But, when they reached the
point of desperation, there was nothing outside of the two of them
and their feelings toward each other that could offer any real relief.
They had to risk going *into* their pain and disappointment before
they could get *through* it to the other side.

Pitfalls and Potentialities of The Romance Stage

Answers: Couples at this early stage of relationship often have a tendency to hope for "the answer" from outside. The partner may be seen as "the answer to my loneliness" or "the answer to my silent prayers." We often tend in the beginning to hope that "things will go easier this time." Easier than they did with my parents, easier than they did with my last partner; easier than they do with other people who don't "love me like you do." What we generally find, however, is that we have to face our inner sense of wanting or questioning in order to discover our "answer." We must reach into and express our hopes and fears, as did Rita and Ron, if we are to reach self-understanding.

Process: This is not to say that romance must always end in pain. Not at all. If couples are willing to risk comfort for the sake of honesty, they may grow gently toward a sense of inner wholeness. If they expect to have it all now, pre-packaged and ready-made, however, they may very well be disappointed. *Intimacy is a process, a journey of disclosing more and more of oneself to another. It is not a product that comes made-to-wear off the shelf.*

Vision: Romance is rightly a time of much hope and expectation. The key is to let our vision *guide us* without losing our sense of what is actually *present within us.* It is the dialogue between our dreams and our "realities" that creates an expanded and fuller sense of reality. A sense of "what is," embroidered with "what could be." Thus, we need romance to give spirit to our often mundane lives. We need to be able to hold within our vision both our ideal and our real selves, if we are ever to actually attain our ideals. As Oscar Hammerstein II reminds us in *South Pacific,* "You gotta have-a dream; If you don't have-a dream, how-ya gonna have-a dream come true?"

Images: "How alike we are!" "How complementary we are!" "What a perfect fit!" "You're just the way I've always dreamed a woman should be!" "You're beyond my wildest dreams!"

Images such as these are often part of the couple's romantic attraction for each other. And at this early stage, to disappoint the partner's image of us may seem to be courting disaster. So, instead of saying how we really feel or think, we may "tint the truth" to a rosier hue, hoping to maintain this glow as long as we can.

The tendency to see one's partner in the best possible light, therefore, may not always be for the best. It may create a pressure on the partner to live up to an image that isn't real. And we, in turn, may pressure ourselves to always be on our "best" behavior. Soon, we have a dialogue between two images rather than between a real-live man and woman.

The process of living up to an image takes a lot of energy. And where does this energy come from? It comes from, or is taken away from, the real-live aspects of the relationship waiting in darkness beneath the surface appearances. Thus, without realizing it, the couple may be feeding the relationship their "images" are having with each other, while starving the *real* relationship potential between them.

Honesty: In order to reverse this image-feeding pattern, one or the other, or preferably both, have to start telling the truth. As in the case of Rita and Ron, they have to reveal something of their hidden selves — not the whole "gunnysack" necessarily, but something real and relevant to the furtherance of their vision.

Sometimes at this stage in a relationship, it becomes "True Confessions" time — with each telling *"everything you ever wanted to know about me but I was afraid you'd never ask so here it is!"*

Quantity, we must remind ourselves, is no substitute for quality. The truth that needs to be told is not so much the *whole* truth as the *relevant* truth — whatever is in our hearts and minds *related to* where we are trying to go together, to our shared vision or mutual aim. Thus, if our aim is to develop a harmonious sexual relationship, I may choose not to disclose details of my past love affairs unless this is in some way truly helpful to our mutual aim. If however, our primary aim is to try to create together a telepathic communication, an ability to see into each other's thoughts, I would not be able to deny any thought that I might be having about some past lover if you asked me about my thoughts.

What's right and true for us at any give time depends upon what we're trying to do together. Our aim may not always be explicit or conscious, however, and we may think we want something and yet see ourselves doing things to sabotage it. When this happens, it's time to wake up and see what's going on with us. It's time to "stop the action," and talk about what we've seen ourselves doing. Admitting to such lapses in awareness may not fit with our image of

We have a dream
a Vision
of where we want to go
together

I dream
our dream
You dream
our dream

Anytime either of us
has a dream
it's really
our dream

Without this inner vision
shared
we easily get lost from our path
or stuck where we are

Sharing this dream
we remind ourselves
that now
is part
of a longer
Presence

competence, but if we wish to take this journey together, we must be willing to stop occasionally to check signals.

What's it all About?

The work of the Romance Stage is the care and tending of a mutual vision, and the development of a sense that we want the same things in a relationship and/or in life. Progress through this stage involves a willingness to communicate about our vision, to take risks to make it happen, and to acknowledge our failures and begin again.

Romance need not be lost when our differences show more clearly and our images fade. It is a quality of hope and positive expectations. And just because our original vision may undergo a number of re-visions along our mutual journey, does not mean that we have lost our dream. A shared aim provides a guiding light for the rockier or steeper parts of the couple's journey. A strongly held romantic vision can greatly strengthen the couple's commitment to stay on course when the going gets rough.

Romance, then, only becomes an *illusion* when we use it to reinforce those aspects of ourselves that would call us to stray from our chosen path. If we want to find out who we *really* are and can be together, we will harness our romantic ideals to achieve that goal.

On page 145, you will find a collection of self-help activities that can be used to further your awareness and growth in the Romance Stage.

TOUCHING

We went for a walk
lightly touching
the misty air of summer rain
we dared not grab
or hold
too tight
the gentle night
told us how to proceed

With care
with care and caution
with care and caution and tiny tremblings
of hope
Excitement
I dared not admit existed

No one knew
what I could not hide
any longer

chapter two

POWER STRUGGLE

(stage II of the couple's journey)

The power struggle emerges after the fall from grace.

It springs from the seeds of disappointment sown by the hands of wishful thinking and selective perceiving. For the struggle to flourish, it requires a soil rich in unacknowledged demands and accumulated resentments. An occasional shower of renewed attempts to simulate lost romantic illusions can increase the yield even more.

The struggle may center on any issue about which we* differ or disagree, but it only becomes a threat to the relationship when one or both of us is consciously or unconsciously engaged in either trying to get the other to be something he or she is not (perhaps trying to make the partner more like one's romantic image), or punishing the partner for being other than one would wish.

---

*A note on the use of "we." I use the subject "we" here and throughout the book as a kind of poetry. I do not expect that everyone will fully identify with every "we!"

FEAR

Everything's just perfect
Too good to be true
Something must be wrong
it must!

I must ferret out the bad
Let's see
What shall I find fault
with first

Well, he's probably too young for me
He's never been in a long-term
serious relationship
And he hasn't developed a commitment
to his career
I fear he's too idealistic to ever
really work at anything

Wow!
I'm really doing it.
I'm really making it wrong
So I can have it.

I'm so afraid
of too much
good

The power struggle arises when hopes or expectations are frustrated, and will continue until we have worked out (via some degree of struggle) a way to satisfy these *or* until we can let go of these expectations *or* until we decide that the discrepancy between what we want and what we've got is large enough to warrant ending the relationship (or altering it significantly).

The power struggle can be valuable as a process of pushing against each other's resistance to change or accomodation in order to develop greater mutual responsiveness. It is often necessary to strongly and persistently assert one's differing wants or needs in order to have them heard by the other. It is not that the partner doesn't *want* to hear, but simply the fact that the two people are different and naturally tend to see the world through the filters of their own wants and needs. Thus, what I'm calling the "power struggle" is an expected, normal step toward the achievement of a relationship where power is balanced and shared.

The Roots of the Power Struggle

The power struggle has its roots in the *individual psyche,* in the *family,* and in *society.* These three systems are complex and interlocking. As I discuss each in turn, I hope their interdependence will be apparent.

The individual psyche. Every individual is born little and helpless into a world of big people. Little vs. big, dependent vs. independent — are primary experiences for all of us. As little people, the world confronts us continually with demands to grow up — if we want our needs met — since the big people around us are never totally dependable. When we're hungry and no one comes to feed us, we feel frustrated and angry. We are dependent on someone else for the fulfillment of this need, and the anger logically should go toward this someone else when we feel it. Unfortunately, as little people, we are not able to clearly differentiate ourselves from our surroundings, so that there is often confusion about where to direct our anger — at mommy or daddy, at ourselves, or at the world in general.

This situation is further complicated by the fact that as we grow from infancy to the toddler stage, we actually become more and more capable of meeting more and more of our needs independently. Thus, while we may *want* mommy or daddy to come and feed us, we no longer *need* this after a time. Still, we feel

TOTAL LOVE

It happens twice
in everyone's life
once when we're small
and once when we're big.

They disappoint us
in some way
big or small
And we begin to see them as ''the other''.

So we take back
the total love
we'd so freely given.
And in taking it back
We no longer have it to give.

And now
it's the third time
or the fourth
or the fifth
or the sixth

And this time
we offer a little less
a little less freely

We hold on
to some of our eggs
so we'll still have some
when the basket breaks.

When the basket breaks —
the illusion —
of total love

We want so much to believe
that human beings can give themselves
whole heartedly

to each other
to work
to a purpose

But we keep discovering
half-hearted midgets
masquerading as lusty, hearty
fully-grown and responsible
men and women.

What stands in the way
of wholehearted action,
commitment,
resolve?

What keeps us half here
and half somewhere else?
Portioning out our eggs:
one for you, one for you, two for you, one for you...

So many competing characters in our dramas:
masculine-feminine, body-mind, oppressor-oppressed,
child-adult, ego-Self.
So many baskets
from which to over-choose.

But there will come a time
in the future-history of our race
when we will see these separate parts
for what they are:
a bunch of little baskets
woven into one, large, all-of-us-included basket
"We're all in the same basket"

Then you will recognize my eggs
as your eggs also
And I will cherish yours
as my own

Mine/Yours
Us/Them
Distinctions so integral
to our present way of thinking

Will dissolve
in total love.

Until then
can we be content
with less-than-perfect love?

I hope so
because that's all I've got to
give you.

frustrated and angry when we don't get our want met. We may even attempt to manipulate the big people to treat us as if we were more helpless than we really are. We may learn to "play helpless" in order to avoid facing the fact that the environment is not always nurturing and that we must learn to "feed" ourselves. Such manipulations never work with people who are themselves independent and self-responsible, but with parents who themselves are still indulging the belief that the world should provide for us, the child may succeed considerably in his or her attempted manipulations. When a little person becomes very successful at playing on the "guilt" of big people, we say that the child is "spoiled" — tyrannical in the expectation of getting his or her own way. Thus, martyr-like parents produce tyrants as children.

And since no parents ever grow up completely secure in their own independence, all children have at least some experience with successful manipulation. There's a bit of the martyr in every parent. There's a bit of the tyrant in every child.

Every one of us comes into adulthood with vestiges of the tyrant child (usually pretty deeply buried) within our psyches. When we marry or enter an intimate relationship, we rekindle the childhood wish to be taken care of: "Maybe my dream really will finally come true!" But as the romantic illusions prove to be just that, once again we are left holding our empty bag of wishes and fantasies — once again feeling alone and frustrated. Disappointment. Unfulfilled expectations. The little tyrant within each of us protests — "No! The world should be more nurturing! I won't accept life on these terms! I will fight to the death to maintain my illusions of a world which revolves around *me!*"

The little tyrant is disappointed over the loss of romantic illusions: "Who is to blame — me or the big people? *They* promised... but maybe I just wasn't good enough..."

The power struggle between intimates grows in part out of the battle between parent and child still smoldering within our own psyches. While the script for this scene was written in our individual nurseries, we can easily plug into one anothers' dramas since all of us have experienced little vs. big, expectation vs. disappointment, blaming vs. self-doubt. And although the details of the *inner* battle vary with each individual, an overall pattern of *external* conflict seems to recur with most couples: one person usually fits most naturally into the tyrannical little person role, while the other obliges by playing the martyred big person; one usually acts out the part of the disappointed one, the other becomes the disappointer; one the blamer, the other, the blamed. We'll take a look at how these roles are "assigned" in the sections on the familial and societal roots of the power struggle, later in this chapter.

There is also a positive, creative aspect of the power struggle with regard to individual psychic development: Two people in an intimate relationship can offer each other both *challenge* and *support* in the development of individual self-responsibility, just as a good parent does. Since we usually welcome *support*, the power struggle will generally revolve around the *challenge*, as we tend to resist challenge to some extent even if it is in the interests of our personal growth.

Dora and Hank — A Classic Power Struggle: Let me quote here from the journal of Dora, one of my clients:

"When I want Hank to 'feed' me — by always being the initiator in our sexual relationship, for example — he will challenge me, saying it's up to me to assert my own wants and not to expect him to always provide for me. This challenge may be 'good for me', but it also hurts. And I will resist this challenge if I feel truly uncertain about my abilities to assert myself sexually. I may even take his *refusal* to feed me as a rejection — countering it with one of those 'if you really loved me ...' song and dances.

We'll be in a power struggle as long as he continues to refuse, while I continue to resist. He may use a variety of power tactics to get me to do what he feels is best for me, him and us: he may coach, coax, cajole, threaten, or ignore me. And I'll use my own arsenal of power tactics: pleading, crying, "trying," acting helpless, or trying to seduce him away from his stance. The impasse persists as long as he continues to challenge me and I refuse to take up the challenge. My *resistance*, due to a real fear of embarking into unknown interpersonal territory, becomes confused with *resentment* toward Hank for not being more helpful — 'for making me grow up!' The parallel between this and the parent-child situation is becoming obvious to me: a parent has to refuse support at times so that the child, and thereby the relationship, can grow. So I ought to thank him for being my teacher, but sometimes that's hard to remember."

Struggles like the one just described are inevitable and necessary to foster individual self-responsibility. The more support which accompanies the challenge, the less resistance there will be, but this may also mean that less psychological "stretching" occurs. Each couple has to determine for itself the proportion of challenge and support appropriate for their particular couple's journey.

Essential to the working through of impasses, however, is the ability on the part of both partners to distinguish *refusal* from *rejection*, and *resistance* from *resentment*. Once Dora became clear that Hank was not *rejecting* her for her lack of sexual initiative but was rather *refusing* to carry the entire responsibility himself, then she knew where she had to focus her attention:

"I had to attend to expanding my range of options — not on winning him back (since he'd never left!). He was simply taking care of himself, not punishing me. This helped me to realize and to help him understand that my *resistance* to change comes from my own fears — not from anger at him (resentment) for his stance. Both of us were responding to our own sense of 'what I have to do for myself'. We really weren't trying to hurt or undermine each other."

When the battle between the sexes can produce learnings such as these, it becomes worth the struggle!

The Roots of the Power Struggle in the Family — *Dora's Story:* Our earliest, and therefore least conscious, learnings about how to be in a relationship usually occur in a family context. You may've been the "baby," "the oldest," "daddy's girl," "mother's little helper," the "peacemaker," or "the black sheep." Whether or not our familial role was as distinctive as one of these, we nevertheless become conditioned to perform certain family roles and avoid others. In Dora's case, she as the eldest of four children, became a "leader" to her brothers and a "helper" to her parents — experiences which influenced greatly her choice of roles in adult love and relationships. This naturally predisposed her toward more of a "dominant," as opposed to submissive position in a man-woman relationship.

Her mother, on the other hand, was the "baby" in a family of six children, while her father's position in his family was generally dominant, as Dora's was.

Dora often saw her parents, Harold and Ruth, portraying the somewhat typical man-woman role relationship: her mother yielding to her father's assertion. Harold would come home from a "hard day at the office" proclaiming his need for some peace and quiet. Ruth would do her best to keep four very active children amused and out of his hair. Or he would move toward her, offering some demonstration of physical affection, to which she would respond warmly-but-shyly, never initiating such overtures toward him, however. They did not have power *struggles* in any overt way. Their relationship simply revealed a power *difference*: he had the power to initiate, she the power to respond. He, the power to ask, she the power to give or to withhold.

Dora often wondered as an adolescent, as her own relationships with boys began to take shape, how satisfied her parents were with their balance of power and roles. To Dora, it seemed a bit restrictive — for them *both*. She wouldn't have wanted to trade places with either of them. She sensed her mother's pain at never having (or taking) the space to initiate or *lead* the direction of the relationship. She sensed her father's wish that her mother would sometimes *take charge* of things — so that he could relax and be led.

While this difference never erupted into a full-scale battle, there was evidence of a kind of struggle going on within each of them and reflected in their relationship to each other. For several years, Harold was on a campaign to help Ruth find her place in the world of work, to help her develop herself in a career — in other words to take a more *active* role in life. At the same time, Ruth was encouraging Harold to *relax* more to allow himself time away from work.

In a sense, this seemed to Dora a power struggle; in another sense it seemed to be a cooperative struggle — each trying to actualize more of their potentials with the other's encouragement. In either case, witnessing her parents' struggles to come to terms with their differences heavily influenced Dora.

These early experiences prepared her for later intimate relationships in several ways: her parents' pattern in some sense provided her with a model of what man-woman relationships look like; their unconscious struggle (to the extent that it *was* unconscious) may've been projected onto her as their child; or in viewing the overt power dynamics in their relationship, Dora could have determined that her life would be *different*. All of these seemed to be operating in her case; let us consider each in turn.

Dora got her basic training for coupling from watching and participating in her parents' relationship. She learned to expect men to behave toward women as leaders, initiators, and dominators. She learned to expect women to behave toward men as followers, accomodaters, and emotional supporters. She saw the man as the provider of structure and material things. She saw the woman as the provider of playfulness, emotionality and spiritual wisdom. The man was somewhat goal-oriented, serious, and critical; the woman more spontaneous, light, and naive. Thus, Dora's preparation for coupling, using her parents as models, gave her a rather stereotypical view of "the way it's supposed to be."

Much psychological case history material, particularly from the work of Jungian theorists, suggests that the parents' "unlived life," i.e., those aspects of their wants, hopes, fears, and resentments which never gain conscious expression, exerts a profound influence on the children. Parents often "project" such unconscious feelings onto their children, with the result that the children "inherit" certain tendencies to behave in ways which seem in opposition to their parents' characteristic ways of being.

Some people try to live up to their parents' expectations. Some try to live them down. Getting caught in either stance keeps one tied to the apron strings. Real self-differentiation is not a rebellious protest.

Although Dora knew this to be true, as an adolescent she spent a lot of energy envisioning how she wanted her relationship to be different from theirs. She didn't want to re-do *their* struggle! She was determined to have her own!

Unsure of her real capacity for equality in a man-woman relationship, for many years she chose to relate to men who were clearly less powerful than she was. In this way, she thought she could guarantee that she would never get into the "one-down" position she'd seen her mother in. Unfortunately, all she guaranteed by this one-sided arrangement was that *she* would be dominant to someone else's submissiveness! There was no equality in this — and therefore no possibility of mutual respect. She was simply repeating her parents' struggle with the sex roles reversed.

It's easy to see how such a power imbalance would endure as long as Dora was still unconsciously re-living her mother's battle with her father, recreating her partner in the image of her father so she could prove her ability to do it *differently* than they had done.

She finally realized that if she was to truly benefit from her mother's legacy to her, she must not only develop a relationship of equality with a man, she must also stand up for those aspects of who she was that she had associated with her mother's "weakness." She slowly began to recognize and communicate the positive aspects of her "feminine" side (e.g., those qualities of emotional yielding and spiritual wisdom she had learned from her mother). She had to stop supressing and start valuing her feminine side if she was to expect similar treatment from a man.

Her goal then became to communicate as well as she could, the strength in her emotional sensitivity and her acceptance of her yielding nature. She found that a man could more easily accept and understand her "weaknesses" when she was communicating these directly rather than trying to live them down. She discovered also that she was suddenly more patient with signs of "weakness" in men, thus enabling them also to actualize their "strength" more fully. As she became less protective of her position of dominance in a relationship, she was able to enjoy new-found, real-live, here-now power in herself and her partner.

Power struggles growing out of a repetition of earlier family patterns will end as the partners learn to live more and more in the here-and-now. This struggle, as it is worked through, will lead us to see that what we are fighting does not actually exist in the present — but is rather a figment of our fantasy-fears based on some earlier experience. In time, Dora came to realize that although she was *like* her mother in some ways, this didn't mean she was destined to repeat her mother's life. Thus, she could *use* what she learned from her mother rather than trying to live it down.

Societal Roots of the Power Struggle: Providing fertile soil for the individual and familial roots of the power struggle is the socially-sanctioned belief — still prevalent in some circles — that men's work makes the world go 'round, while women are meant to keep men happy so they can continue to do the work of the world.

The story goes like this: "It is the man's role to provide materially for his family. Thus, he must be concerned with getting the job done; he must be task-oriented and goal-focused if he is to be adequate in this role. It is the woman's role to provide emotionally for her family. Thus, she must be concerned with maintaining harmony in interpersonal relationships.

The man's *goal*-centeredness can cause him at times to act quickly and decisively without too much regard for the emotional consequences.

The woman's *relationship*-centeredness leads her at times to try to attend to both sides of a potential conflict in order to harmonize the situation. This often slows down progress toward the goal and creates inefficiency in the eyes of those who are more task-oriented.''

Even in today's climate of women's and men's liberation, these themes are very present in the groups I lead — whether in a work setting or in a family context. The most pressing issue I hear from men is "how can I afford to relax or become less goal-oriented! If I don't achieve my goals, I'm seen as a failure — not only by society but by my family as well!''

And from women, especially married women who work, I hear, ''I can't really give free reign to my ambition and creativity. This might interfere with providing a nurturing, supportive climate for my loved ones, and then I'd be seen as inadequate as a women!''

Thus, both men and women are threatened by social disapproval if they do not live up to their prescribed functions.

Given the contrasting role expectations for men and women in our culture, it is easy to see how conflicts and ultimately power struggles, can arise: *Her* "Concern with people's feelings" can get in the way of *His* "getting the job done." *His* emphasis on "efficiency and control" can interfere with *Her* needs to "give audience to the feelings of all concerned." Even if their more essential natures want to rebel against this state of affairs, they often feel trapped by it.

In organizational settings, also, I have talked with men and women about their opinions regarding male vs. female supervisors. Here, too, the socially-based power struggle continues. Women leaders who tend to favor more relationship-centered styles are often labeled (by both men and women) as "compromising," "wishy-washy," or "indecisive," while if they lean toward more task-oriented styles, they are labeled "domineering" or even "ball-busting." (See my research article entitled "Women and Success" in Volume 1, #1 *Humanistic Psychology Institute Review*, Fall 1978.) Thus, it seems they "can't win" if they have chosen the atypical cultural role of women leaders.

Opinions of male supervisors reveal a complementary range of negative stereotypes: Men who tend to be task-oriented leaders are labeled "rigid," "controlling," and "insensitive;" while the more democratic types are often criticized as being "unable to take a stand," or even "cowardly." It's hard to believe that in this age of heightened social awareness, men are still compared against the macho get-the-job-done ethic, while women are evaluated in terms of their ability to be nurturing and attractive. Old beliefs die slowly.

Although there is an attempt to balance task achievement and relationship values, power and love, technology and ecology in our world, the battle rages on. And it is this struggle between basic values in our society that underlies the battle of the sexes.

Until men are supported in relaxing some of their goal-directedness; and until women are encouraged to take more leadership in the world of material goals and tasks, men and women will be hampered in developing real empathy for one another — empathy being only the first step toward the recognition that we're not so different after all. We've simply been differentially conditioned to focus on one-half of society's work and to leave the other half to our partner.

Thus, man-woman power struggles are not simply an individual matter. We are each fighting for our rights to be more than society has taught us to be. And we are fighting also to bring to the culture a more flexible or androgynous assignment of roles so that together, as men and women, we can go beyond the power struggle to a stage in our cultural evolution where power and love are valued equally.

The Anatomy of Spite

No matter what the origin of a couple's power struggle, whether rooted in the individual personality, the family history, or the culture, we sometimes see situations where the couple seem stuck where they are.

When the struggle continues for a long period unabated, it tends to assume more and more subtle proportions. It may even develop into a "spite war," as illustrated by this excerpt from Dora's journal:

"Hank and I no longer fight about whether I'm as much of a turn on as some previous lover. Now, he just signals that this question is in his mind by mentioning someone from his past, after which I signal that this has registered with me by mentioning one of my old flames (my message being, 'He knew how to love me — why can't you?')

The other night our little tilt had even more hidden dimensions: he insulted my taste in clothes, after which I promptly went and got dressed, putting on an outfit which he'd recently told me he hated."

The messages in these sorts of "conversations" are rarely

missed, although rarely spoken directly.

What is Spite? Spite is the height of passive aggressiveness. You hit me (or I imagine that you have), so I hit you back. Tit for tat. Do unto others what they've done to you. Have the last word. But do it subtly, as passively as possible, so you can't be held responsible for it.

Spite arises from the pits of the lowest, the most selfish and competitive, aspect of human nature. It's a weapon that might be necessary if life were a jungle — which it isn't unless we treat it as one.

Still, the vestiges of our animal natures are with us, for better or for worse. And in pursuing a deep, intimate relationship (with the self-confrontation that this entails), we often find that "the closer s/he gets, the worse you look". This is because as a relationship develops, growing in security and trust, we naturally risk revealing more and more of the hidden or "shadow" sides of our personalities. It's a kind of testing of the limits of the relationship, the key question being "how much of myself can I dare to reveal to this other person — without causing too much stress on the relationship?" The "demons" in our personalities exert pressure toward expression. And the more we try to hide them, the more sinister and uncontrollable is their force. Still, we cannot "blow the lid off" Pandora's box, since a relationship needs to grow in its ability to manage conflict before it can constructively use these potentially-creative/potentially-destructive demonic forces.

Spiteful behavior can serve as a kind of indicator of the amount of underlying conflict between two people. Its existence can be denied or confronted depending on their commitment and ability to deal with conflicts. Sometimes spiteful behavior can be noted by one or both people but not confronted until a later date when the relationship has developed more reliable means for communicating, checking out perceptions and resolving differences. However, if it remains too long under the surface (in the "unconscious") of the relationship, it will grow like a cancer, consuming the entire relationship.

Thus, spite is a symptom of buried conflict. It stems from a **competitive, "me vs. you," view of human interaction. Such a view, in the building of a trusting relationship, often must be tested before it can be overcome.**

Chronic and Acute Spite: **The presence of spite wars can be seen** as a developmental phase to be resolved over time as the relationship grows in trust and commitment; or they may indicate that a conflict which was at one time out in the open has gone "underground," due to frequent impasses in trying to resolve it. It is important to know which is which. If we treat a *chronic* spite war (one of long-standing that has gone underground) as simply a phase to be resolved (an "*acute* attack," we might call it), then we are denying the fact that a radical change is needed in the way the couple deals with conflict. On the other hand, if an *acute* attack of spite gets mistaken for more than it is, the couple could become overly vigilant in the matter and begin to see every expression of difference as a spiteful act.

Julia and Emmett — Acute Spite Attacks: Julia and Emmett have been together for 9 years. Up until quite recently Julia has centered her life around Emmett and their two small daughters. Now that the girls have started school and Julia has more time to herself, she is beginning to recognize that she actually cherishes this newly discovered alone time. She has started to write poetry and is keeping a journal of her inner thoughts and feelings — things she'd often dreamed of doing but never had the time for when the children were at home all day. Emmett, a painter whose studio is at home, had looked forward to the time when the kids would be away for part of the day so that he and Julia could spend more intimate time together. At first, when Julia would choose to be alone rather than with him, he acted hurt and angry, accusing her of "drifting away" from him. After several of these encounters where Julia assured him that all she wanted was an hour or two a day of alone time, Emmett seemed to accept her need as reasonable. They stopped fighting and the problem seemed to be solved. As time passed, however, Julia noticed that Emmett was spending more and more time in his studio — with the door closed — something which had in the past signaled his absolute need for privacy.

Julia was disturbed by this and after several weeks got up the courage to ask him about it. When confronted with the discrepancy between what he *said* he wanted and what he was doing, Emmett was forced to look critically at his behavior. He realized that he had felt powerless in Julia's decision to spend more time alone and the only way he could regain a feeling of control over his life was to do something about that part of his life which excluded Julia — his work. He'd gotten more involved in his work as a reaction to Julia getting more involved in her inner thoughts and writing. In "spite language," it was as if he were saying, "ok for you — you *want* alone time? I'll *give* you alone time. I'll give you so much of it that you'll wish you'd never wanted it!''

Fortunately, Emmett was open and non-defensive enough to admit to his hurt feelings and his attempt to gain a feeling of power through spite. (This was partly aided by Julia's non-accusatory way of broaching the issue. Her first words went something like, ''I don't see enough of you these days...'' rather than ''Why do you **always hide from me in your studio?!''**)

Once out in the open, the conflict situation could be renegotiated. Emmett and Julia could look again at each other's needs in light of their needs as a couple. Emmett was able to see that, the way their time had been structured up to now, he'd actually had about twice as much time to himself as Julia did. In the early days of the marriage, Emmett had not expected Julia to need as much time alone as he did. Thus, the marriage had started out with this expectation, based on their needs at that time. When this new need emerged for Julia, he was unsure about how to interpret it. Did it mean, for example, that she was finding him less interesting or attractive? Emmett's acceptance of responsibility for his questions and feelings gave Julia the chance to clarify the meaning of the change in her behavior. It gave them both a chance to mutually agree on the amount of time each wanted to spend together vs. alone. As it happened, the two found that they *both* had greater needs for alone time than they thought ''appropriate'' for married people. They realized that they had been using this ''crisis'' as a way of secretly — rather than openly — bargaining for what they wanted.

As the couple got their concerns out in the open, they began to understand that normal changes in family life (the birth of a baby, the entrance of a child into school) introduce reverberating changes in the other parts of the family ''system''. With this information in mind, they were now able to anticipate problems rather than being caught off-guard by them. They came to value approaching these rites of passage consciously, seeing them as opportunities to renegotiate their mutual expectations and to expand their response-ability.

In this particular conflict situation, each was able to look at old expectations and new needs in a way that respected change as a normal part of living together. The children's entrance into school brought on a change in Julia's need for alone time, which led to a change in Emmett's feelings about her commitment, and

GAMES

Who is this man
of my unacknowledged dreams?

Is he like the others?

Will he dominate me?
Will he be dominated?

Will he take care of me?
Will he require that I take care of him?
Will he let me take care of him?

Will he be confused by my confusion?
Will his confusion bring me down?

Does he want me?

Can he love me?

Each question is like a hypothesis
to be tested
And the experimental design
is a game

A game where only one of us
knows the rules
and the stakes

Where it's up to the other one of us
to find out
thereby ending
the game

and possibly
the relationship

consequent retaliatory changes in *his* need for alone time. His spiteful actions and her recognition of these brought about further changes in the couple's way of handling disappointment or unmet expectations — namely, they learned to decipher the garbled messages conveyed by spiteful acts instead of being mystified and allowing them to escalate.

The case of Julia and Emmett illustrates an *acute* rather than a *chronic* case of spite. Spite, in this case, was used as an attempt to re-establish equilibrium in the couple's power system following a family developmental crisis, which they were confronting for the first time. Thus, they were not indulging in spite according to a long-standing, recurring pattern. The acute type could have become chronic if Emmett's first act of spite had been followed by a corresponding spite on Julia's part, which would then lead to retaliation by Emmett, escalation by Julia, and on and on.

David and Virginia — A Chronic Spite War: The solution to a chronic spite pattern requires a more rigorous and disciplined approach. The case of David and Virginia Woodward illustrates such a chronic spite situation. David and Virginia had been married 25 years, since both were 19 and just graduated from high school. At Central High, David had been president of the student council and very popular, while Virginia, although a good student, received little recognition for her talents. Early on, David adopted the more dominant position in the relationship. While in the early days, Virginia generally acceded to David's wishes, as time went on she gradually began to speak her own mind more and more. Unfortunately, David found it hard to be with a woman who differed with or contradicted him, even if it only occurred occasionally. He began to speak more and more often about wanting her to be a "graceful lady," or sometimes simply "how nice it would be to be with a graceful lady!" Virginia of course, caught the message. And being "eager to please" (the other side of the coin of spite), she vowed to become the "graceful lady" of David's fantasy. She began to speak to David only when she could say something gentle or harmonious, and to refrain from subjects and style of speech which could be in any way abrasive, displeasing, or confrontive. Thus, she showed him how *totally* graceful she could be. Which should've pleased him. Or should it?

He became increasingly uncomfortable over the next few years as Virginia continued to "please" him. Everything he did, she supported. When he decided to expand his business, even though it would take much of his free time and the couple's financial resources to accomplish this, she agreed that this would be best for the family's security in the long run. When he began to spend more and more time on the road marketing his products, she accommodated by helping him out in the local branch office.

He feigned appreciation of her efforts and chastized himself for not being more honestly grateful. As this pattern continued, he felt more and more shoddy and selfish. The more she acceded to his every demand, the shoddier he felt. He began gradually to develop an impulse to retaliate, continuing to increase his self-oriented demands. Before long his business and recreational needs became the focal point around which nearly all family activities revolved. These developments simply provided newer and more challenging opportunities for Virginia to display her "gracefulness". Which of course pushed David farther and deeper into the hole of his retaliatory selfishness.

This chronic pattern was taking place during the 20-year period when the Woodwards were raising their three children. When the youngest child left home to go to college, they found themselves alone in the house with each other. In this environment the couple began to experience an intensification of their negative feelings toward one another, which they could no longer use the children to help buffer.

Gradually, Virginia became less graceful and more bitchy, having realized that the payoff for her graceful accommodations had actually amounted to nothing more than an increase in David's spiteful selfishness. She began to see her life as wasted. She'd given up her life to provide "harmonious companionship" for David. Now, when they had the chance to really share this companionship, they were finding they truly despised one another. Her disappointment was overwhelming — she became depressed and weepy for days on end, saying to David only, "I'm so disappointed...It's all your fault."

Her combination of helpless depression and blaming was a difficult pattern for David to cope with, let alone challenge. He felt somehow guilty and yet somehow unjustly accused. Since Virginia's weepy complaints gave him little space for feeling anger at her accusations, he "decided" to act out the *guilt* rather than the *anger* — since that's what *she was asking for!*

David adopted the guilty and ashamed "How-can-I-ever-make-it-up-to-you?" posture, complete with promises for a better life if only she'd take him back. Virginia recognized, however, that if she *let* David "make it up to her," he once again would be on top, and she underneath. Virginia was not going to give up her role as "victim" too quickly.

For almost two years David and Virginia tolerated each other in this chronic spite pattern: she feeling constantly depressed and despairing about the worthlessness of her life, and he feeling guilty and attempting to make her happier by suggesting things she might do or by initiating trips, outings, or other shared recreation. The "Why don't you (or we)... Yes but..." game. Over and over and over and over. Until finally David realized he had become very, very tired. He was tired of being on top — initiating, taking charge, solving problems. And he was beginning to hear that this was exactly what Virginia had been complaining about — that he always ran things and she always followed his lead. Her depression was her way of mourning this fact, experiencing her impotence, and punishing him — all at once.

As he saw this more and more clearly, he became depressed over his own life. He saw how "wrong" he'd been all these years and vowed to stop initiating and start taking his lead from her. After all, this is what she'd been crying about for these past couple of years, wasn't it?

Now, David felt he'd *finally* seen the light — after groping his way through a 22-year tunnel. He proudly announced to Virginia that from now on what they did with their time and money, where they went on trips, when and if they had sexual relations — were *all* up to her! She would finally be the victim no longer. *She* could run things for a change.

Virginia received David's announcement with very mixed emotions. What autonomy did she really have when he was telling her she now *had to* take charge of everything — whether she wanted to or not! And besides, her 22-plus years of training for the underling role had scarcely prepared her for this sudden "freedom". She told him she'd like to be able to accept his "generous" offer, but that she didn't really *have* any wants of her own, since she'd been shaped over the years into being a "graceful lady" rather than an assertive woman with her own separate ideas, feelings, and wants. David was understandably puzzled. He had thought that since the "cause" of Virginia's problem had been his dominance in their relationship, the logical solution would be for him to become submissive for a change — so she would have nothing to be unhappy with!

Unfortunately, the solution was not this simple. Twenty-two years on the spite merry-go-round had made them both so dizzy that they no longer knew when they were *acting* from their own wants and when they were *reacting* in order to have a particular effect on their partner. They agreed that they were at an impasse, and decided to seek the assistance of a counselor.

A first stage in the counseling process was to help the couple see themselves and their situation more clearly and to accept *responsibility* for mutually creating it. Then, we worked to expand their range of *choices* for responding to the situation, so they could get themselves out of the tangled web they were in. Through this process, they came to consciously experience for the first time their absolute *interdependence,* both in creating and in changing the situation. They felt what it means to be "in relationship," a first step toward the experience of interdependent wholeness, which is the aim of the couple's journey. Each also developed a much expanded sense of individual identity, and saw how self-actualization and relationship growth can be complementary aspects of a whole.

As David and Virginia began to search for a way back to the path toward wholeness, they used the "safety" of the consulting room to escalate their cold war into a heated battle.

David began by attacking Virginia for creating a "damned if you do, damned if you don't" situation for him — the epitomy of spite, he thought. Virginia countered by asserting that she, too, felt in a double bind. She was being *told* to initiate — an act that she saw as pure paternalism. The web of spite/counter-spite in which these two seasoned battlers were entangled became painfully obvious.

The first task was to help each to recognize that they were *co-equally* responsible for the situation. They each needed to feel their own pain, as well as how each was doing things to spite (and therefore cause pain to) the other.

While such insight/awareness is a necessary first step, it is not enough to bring about behavior change. Both persons are engaging in the pattern because *it is all they know how to do.* In order for change to occur, each must learn a new way of *being in the relationship.* In this instance, it was clear that each had become encased in a rigid sex-typed role definition which over the years had become increasingly polarized. They themselves had "prescribed" correctly: a more assertive role for Virginia and a less directive role for David. Their way of arriving at this plan, however, had been entirely too rigid and all-or-nothing. For a real role expansion to take place, Virginia would have to initiate — *in her own way* — not according to David's directive. And for a real change in David's behavior to occur, he would have to feel the need to give up control — from the depths of his own feeling of bewilderment, not out of a need to "help Virginia". In other words, a lessening of David's over-directiveness would have to grow from a genuine feeling of not knowing which way to go.

A chronic spite pattern in which each partner plays a rigidly stereotyped role can best be broken by expanding the behavioral range of each. Thus, in counseling, I sought to give attention to the part of each of them which was being ignored: Virginia's feelings of assertiveness and David's feelings of helplessness. Such new feelings do not arise fully developed, waiting for the therapist's validation, obviously. Only tiny hints are present in the beginning.

Virginia's "bitchiness," provided the first clue to her potential assertiveness. She knew about the part of her that *didn't want* what she was getting. Perhaps in time, she could learn about the part of her that *did* want some things, too. David's feelings of guilt, of "where did I go wrong?", although still reflecting his paternalistic attitude, at least showed a degree of self-questioning, a glimmer of acceptance of responsibility. These were the building blocks for beginning the resolution of the impasse. As I continued to probe and thereby validate Virginia's criticalness, she recognized more and more the power in her own feelings and perceptions. As she was encouraged to risk being "un-graceful" by expressing these, she was able to clarify and refine her confused irritation into cogent anger and self-assertion.

In order not to allow Virginia to simply dump on her unsuspecting (or at least unprepared) husband, and to help prepare him to sustain the beating he was getting, I formed a different sort of coalition with David. I directed him to consciously *try* to experience self-doubt in response to Virginia's challenges. This allowed David to remain in control of his feelings — since he was *trying* to do something difficult that would be *helpful* to the therapy. David's pride needed the added assurance that he was trying the new posture in order to help the situation, and although I never specifically reinforced this attitude, I allowed David to keep it, knowing that sooner or later he would give it up of his own volition.

Over the course of 6 months of therapy, Virginia's bitchiness mellowed into some very astute perceptions about David, herself, and their relationship. She began to tell, at first somewhat harshly and later more carefully, what she did and did not like about the way he behaved toward her. David began to feel stupid for failing to recognize the perceptiveness of this woman with whom he'd shared life for nearly 23 years. He began to sit up and notice, and to shut up and listen. As she became more confident in her assertiveness, he could allow himself to feel a little bit "out of control." Formerly, when he'd seen her as a child, or as the graceful lady of his own creation, he'd felt he had to be in control at all times — since *she* surely wasn't. Now, however, he actually felt tinges of respect, even awe. He began to experience the "child" in himself — an aspect of his personality that wanted to be taken by the hand and led. But this time, he was not asking to be led by another child — as had occurred when he'd insisted that Virginia take charge when she was yet totally unprepared to do so. Now, Virginia had some confidence that she could sometimes be a guiding support for David's "child". Slowly, David experimented with his newly-discovered "helplessness", allowing Virginia to tell him what she wanted and how she was experiencing him. He did not give up control totally — which would've been expecting too much support from another person. He learned how to feel and express uncertainty, without collapsing completely under its weight.

Virginia, in complementary fashion, learned to assert her feelings without giving up the tentativeness she knew so well. She did not become arrogant about her new-found power. David's genuine need and respect for her gave her the sense of *responsibility* to use her power carefully.

The operation was a success. After 22 years of chronic spite and 1½ years of hard work to reverse this pattern, David and Virginia began again. They had found their way back to the path. They had used the raw materials of their power struggle to develop beyond the struggle to an experience of shared power. David discovered that by supporting Virginia's emerging assertiveness, and allowing his own tender feelings to emerge, he gained more freedom to be himself in the relationship. Virginia discovered that by accepting David's more tender aspects and at the same time expressing her own feelings and wishes, she had a renewed feeling of commitment to the relationship. Together, they were able to return again to their place of beginning and, as T.S. Eliot's famous lines describe, "to know it for the first time."

The power struggle results in a decision by the couple to stay together or to separate. Although, as David and Virginia discovered, contact with the other has brought pain, the partners may have a great deal to contribute to one another's development. On the other hand, they may be at odds with regard to basic values or lifestyle orientations — one oriented toward the world of material *things*, for example, while the other focuses his or her life around living *beings*. Or we may find our basic "rhythms" are very discrepant, his need for a great deal of privacy, contrasting with her need for a lot of attention and interaction. In cases of such basic value or rhythm conflicts, it may be very costly to try to hang on to each other.

The power struggle also generally results in a workable set of rules for negotiating conflicts between self and other and between us and the world. Roles, goals, communication channels, and decision-making processes have been tested and established.

Trust now becomes more a question of "I trust you to act according to your conscience" rather than "I trust you not to do anything to displease me", since now couples have learned some essential lessons: (1) they cannot control or change one another by an act of will; (2) love cannot be demanded, (3) they can survive pain and disappointment; and (4) they are two separate unique individuals with two separate unique sets of needs, goals and rhythms.

Thus, again, we see the chief lesson of the *Couples Journey*: as long as we stay on the path and keep working to more deeply understand our current experience, it will change and emerge into something else. The landscape of the journey will grow continually richer, as we become more able to see and experience our present place on the path.

On page 148 you will find a collection of self-help activities that can be used to further your awareness of Power Struggle issues.

TAKING SPACE & MAKING SPACE

In any relationship
one person will have a clearer sense of self
than the other —
firmer boundaries,
a more sharply differentiated internal structure,
a more orderly personal style;
this person will play the "taking space" role;
this person is often a He;

The other person —
the one with more fluid boundaries,
with a less sharply defined internal structure
and a more flexible personal style —
will play the "making space" role;
this person is often a She.

The "space taker," because he has a more
defined structure, is less apt to be
"distracted" by data or events which
don't fit the pre-ordained structure
and he can therefore decide and act more
quickly and with more force and certainty.

The "space maker" because she has
a more flexible structure, is more
apt to be "distracted" by data or events which
don't fit neatly
into the structure
she therefore takes more time to decide
and her actions are less forceful and more tentative.

The space taker will always appear to be
the more dominant one,
the more assertive one.

The space maker will appear to be
more compliant,
more accomodating

The space taker may resent the space maker
for letting him dominate, for moving too slowly, for giving
him too much room, thus
making him feel insecure.

The space maker may resent the space taker
for dominating, for moving too quickly, for not giving her
enough space to feel and assert her wants, thus
making her feel powerless.

The space taker may get anxious
in the face of too much space; he may
project into this vacuum his own worst fears
of what she wants or is feeling.

The space maker may get anxious about
having too little space; she may feel encroached upon
by his anxiety-provoked projections and resist him.
Or she may make space for
(and thus accomodate to) his projected fears,
and behave as if these projections were her own
inner feelings.

In either instance, the space maker gives up her freedom
to create her own self-definition,
her own inner structure.
She succumbs to the outer demand
to "hurry up and do something"
instead of responding to the inner need
to develop her self-definition
out of the variety of seemingly chaotic forces
alive in her psyche.

(This tendency is reinforced
by a technology-oriented social structure

which values efficiency and de-values "disorderliness".)

*The space taker identifies so strongly with the cultural norm
that he ignores those aspects of his own being
that would require him to stop and listen.*

*Thus, he like Popeye comes to believe,
"I am what I am and that's all that I am"
— rarely pausing to look beneath the surface.*

*This short-circuited approach to "selfhood"
leaves their deeper natures undeveloped
and unavailable for a mutual give and take relationship.*

*He resents her
for failing to bring her full self into the relationship
for forcing him to take more than his share
of the responsibility.*

*She resents him
for taking up so much space in the relationship
that there seems to be not enough space or time
for the various impulses in her psyche to be felt
and formed into a coherent response.*

*He hates her for being witholding.
She hates him for being overbearing.*

Isn't it a pity

that he can't learn
    to make space
so she can learn
    to take space
	that she can't learn
	    to take space
	so he can learn
	    to make space

chapter three

STABILITY

(stage III of the couple's journey)

After romance has blossomed and matured, after power has been tested, and equality achieved, couples come to the third stage in the journey, *stability*.

Stability represents not sameness or continual peace so much as an attitude of *acceptance:* acceptance of the other as a real, live separate *other*, who may not always meet my expectations; and acceptance of the parts of myself that create such expectations.

The Calm After the Storm

Stability is a stage of looking inward (into myself) instead of outward (at the other) for the source of conflicts. I come to understand that our differences and struggles during the Power Struggle Stage are also a mirror of my own inner struggles. Our disagreements about your wish for more "freedom" in the relationship and my wish for "security" are partly outer expressions of my *inner* conflict, my own wish for both freedom and security. As long as such conflicts are unresolved *within* me, they will be expressed as conflicts *between* us.

THE RE-VISION

Do I feel secure enough
to let him feel secure enough
to go away from me when he chooses
to be with others when he chooses
to get totally involved in his work when he chooses
and to come back to me when he chooses?

Do I feel secure enough
to let him know I'll be here
when he comes back?

or not to be here sometimes
if that's what I want?

And do I feel secure enough
to want to please him
without having to,
to want him to please me
without having to get my way

to recognize needs that he doesn't meet in me
without punishing him for it

to acknowledge my limitations in meeting his needs
without expecting or provoking
his punishment?

Can I show him how secure I am
without making him feel superfluous
without denying my fleeting insecurities
without forgetting how much I want him?

And can I feel how much I want him
without feeling insecure?

My work in the Stability Stage, therefore, is to take responsibility for the conflict or ambivalence as existing within me. And yours likewise is for your own inner work. As we continue to discuss our differences, I come eventually to accept that part of you that I may have wished to change. This may occur in at least two ways: (1) perhaps I realize that no matter what I try, I cannot change you, and thus, as I accept some hated or feared part of you, I am more able to see and accept that part in me (such as my wish for more "freedom"). What used to threaten me about you, I come to own as mine also. And with this greater ownership, comes familiarity, and a lessening of the threat; or (2) as I continue to observe you, myself, and us over time, I come to see that sometimes I want security and you want freedom (for example), while other times these preferences are reversed. I begin to see that my "identifications" (which *part* of myself I identify as "me") change like the weather. Realizing this, I gain a more stable perspective on the continual comings and goings of our various parts.

Stability is born out of living with the awareness of change. We have seen the futility of "hanging on to a position," which characterized some of our power struggles. And we have experienced how letting go of a rigidly-held position and allowing a new awareness to enter us is an act of courage rather than compromise.

During the Stability Stage, we must become careful observers of these changing "sub-personalities:" today I'm the nurturing parent; yesterday I was like a helpless child; and tomorrow I may be "someone" entirely new!

We now use conflicts and disagreements as opportunitites for learning about ourselves, rather than as chances to win points. Stability encourages a deepened awareness of who we are beyond our daily, ever-changing moods or identifications. We are learning to accept the relationship even with its ups and downs — "to ride the roller coaster in the direction in which it's going." We know we've arrived at this stage when we can have such perspective on a fight or disagreement that we feel, "here is another opportunity for learning more about ourselves."

We've "survived" the power struggles and are stronger for the experience. We know our potential for hurting and our tolerance for being hurt. We know how much conflict and individualism the relationship can handle, and we agree not to push these limits

I am finally ready to admit
that I don't prefer to be with you
"all the time" (like in Johnny Mathis' song)
and that you feel that way too

that I'm not always open to you sexually (just most of the
*   time!)*
as you're not always open to me

that sometimes I don't even like you
and sometimes you don't like me

This feels a little like a confession
But it's also an invitation:
let's stop pretending
let's stop trying
let's stop manipulating ourselves
let's stop suffering.

carelessly. We can also see how some of our relationship struggles grow out of our individual habits: "Everytime you tell me what you want in bed, I get the feeling I've done something wrong! I lose my erotic feelings, and tend to withdraw." We see such events as *parts* of a larger whole, not to be taken too seriously. We have more perspective now, and are less likely to become hurt or discouraged by any single event.

We notice a certain predictability to our "ups and downs." Seeing our pattern of contact and withdrawal or conflict and resolution allows us to feel peaceful and calm deep inside, even while experiencing a heated argument.

Repeating the same power struggles over and over, and learning with each repetition to resolve the conflict a little more quickly or cooperatively, leads to more confidence in our ability to nourish and forgive ourselves and each other. We see the connections between our individual habit patterns and their roots in our childhood relationships with parents, and thereby understand our struggles as not only *between* you and me but also *within* each of us. Such struggles represent the conflict between my "internalized *parent*" and the *child*-I-used-to-be-but-still-carry-with-me. The "internal-ized parent" is that aspect of one's personality which "carries on the work" of one's real parent, treating one as if still a child in need of parental guidance.

Through this process of growth and learning, we each begin to take responsibility for whatever lessons life brings. We stop blaming each other and start focusing on the power struggles within

Carla and Henry — The "Sleeping Beauties": Couples can move through the power struggle to the stability stage by recognizing and taking charge of an archaic habit pattern in which they seem to be stuck.

Carla and Henry were in their late twenties and had been living together for four years when they came for counseling. They presented their problem as a difficulty in openly communicating their sexual love even though they both felt tremendously attracted to one another. He wished that she would be more aggressive in their lovemaking in order to help him overcome his fear of initiating sex. She wished that *he* would be the aggressor in order to help her feel that she was wanted or desirable. Each was waiting for the other to make the first move. Thus, not much was happening for these young lovers!

It's a dry period
The days are gray
but without enough energy
even to rain

Moisture locked up
Juices in reserve
Not a storm in sight

Just a peaceful
time for withdrawing
each into our own
separate cloud

But because I remember
how it was
not so long ago,
I can sit
with my freeze-dried feelings
waiting for our water to boil again
heating up my hunger
whetting my appetite
melting my tears of longing
re-kindling a storm
of needs, hopes, and plans

Because we remember
how warm and juicy it was
it still is
and always will be
as long as we remember

Though they entered counseling in the heat of the Power Struggle stage, even their arguments showed little passion. They were both passively resisting any attempt by the partner to manipulate them into action. Each had a clear mental picture of what she or he would respond to, and each was relentless in attempts to cajole the partner into the required behavior. Their bedroom scene looked like two sleeping beauties, lying motionless side-by-side waiting for prince or princess charming to come along and bestow the magic kiss that would set the interaction in motion.

Carla's "withholding" made Henry feel rejected. Henry's "passivity" made Carla feel unloveable. Each was aware that in order for the distance between them to be bridged, *someone* had to make the first move. But, since each took the other's self-protective pattern as a personal *rejection*, it was hard to risk further rejection by reaching out!

Carla and Henry needed a new perspective, one which showed each partner to be *in genuine need of the other's help,* rather than manipulating each other to do what each ought to be able to do alone. To help them gain that improved view, we began a series of individual Gestalt Therapy-style dialogues* between Carla and her "internalized parents" and between Henry and his "parents" — each dialogue occurring in a joint session, with the partner as witness.

In Carla's dialogue with her mother, it became apparent that even though Carla presented herself as a confident and somewhat assertive woman, she had an internalized mother who was shy, withdrawn and unsure of her sexual attractiveness. Indeed, her own mother *was* shy, fearful and uncomfortable with her own sexuality.

Carla's dialogues with her "father" revealed a man who, while respecting and loving his daughter for her achievements, feared his attraction to her sexually, and therefore cut off all expressions of

---

*In Gestalt therapy-style dialogue, a person sits facing an empty chair and "imagines" another person (e.g., one's parent or spouse) to be sitting there. After talking to this imaginary person, one then switches chairs and "becomes" the other, addressing oneself. This dialogue with the "empty chair" can continue until closure or illumination of the issue is reached. It is a way of helping one to become conscious of, or "own," an aspect of the self that has formerly been unconscious ("dis-owned" or "projected" onto another, such as one's partner). It is often used, as with Henry and Carla, to facilitate awareness of parental relationships and attitudes which strongly influence current behavior patterns.

physical affection toward her when she was quite young.

Thus, Carla's life experience contained a large "hole" where validation of her sexuality was concerned. She needed to learn to fill this hole herself in order to overcome her passivity with Henry. There were some ways Henry could help in this, if he was willing, and if he could get from her some clues as to *how*.

Unfortunately, as is often the case, Henry had his own set of "holes" in the development of *his* sexuality. His therapeutic "dialogues" with his internalized mother revealed a woman who feared losing control of her son and who used her sexuality as a tool for manipulating his compliance. When he conformed, she would appreciate him; when he disagreed or differed with her, she would punish him by withholding affection. Thus, he learned to be wary of becoming involved with a woman, lest she manipulate him into compliance and reject him when he tried to differentiate himself. His "inner source of mothering" (and therefore his ability to nurture or give mothering to himself) was mistrusted and viewed with caution. Thus, he had great difficulty *receiving* mothering from another. Any woman had to prove herself to be unconditionally loving, non-controlling, and able to tolerate differentness in order to win his trust. And Carla, after all, was a mere human being!

Henry's internalized father was a somewhat shadowy, unemotional figure who seemed to be under the control of his wife and reluctant to support Henry in his struggles against her. Thus, Henry was forced at an early age to fight his battles for independence and nurturance without much parental support. Henry came to see his needs for nurturance as a distinct liability in relating to females. He developed a habit of seeking closeness with a woman via *her* dependency (or "neediness") rather than his own.

Henry began to see himself more clearly after the "internal parent" dialogues. He recognized how his "picture" of women interfered with receiving love from a real woman. Carla, likewise could more readily own her struggle between the fear of initiating and the fear of being rejected: this was *her inner conflict* as well as a conflict between her and Henry. Watching Henry own his equal responsibility in creating this situation helped her to accept her part in it.

Thus, Carla and Henry moved from "blame and self-doubt," characteristic of the power struggle, to "mutual learning," a key attitude in the Stability Stage. Carla and Henry became aware of both sides of themselves: each wished to *receive* nurturance "without having to ask," and each wished to *give* to the other.

When a couple accepts such equal responsibility for creating their situation, power struggles dissolve into mutual problem-solving adventures. Once Henry could see that he really needed Carla's help in learning to trust a woman, he was more able to receive such help. And once Carla could see the type of help Henry needed, and could feel him actually reaching out to her, she was moved from her self-protective stuck-place to a willingness to make "the first move" (Perhaps actually the *second* move, in response to Henry's expression on need, but who's counting anymore?!).

In Henry's words: "We've openly faced our anxieties about impotence and unloveability. We no longer need to avoid the pain of these experiences. We've seen our own and each other's shadow sides and come away intact."

Henry and Carla faced their resistance to *staying with* a painful situation. They confronted their desire to run and hide...and managed to stay. No one *won* the power struggle, and therefore both *survived* it — experiencing a fuller appreciation of both pain and joy in the process. They recognized and appreciated each other more for the tremendous act of will and self-discipline this required.

A major task of the Stability Stage is to develop such self-disciplined ability to stay engaged in a painful situation until a wider perspective is gained. Instead of a knee-jerk identification with "my side" vs. "your side," we each step back and look at both sides. As we mature in this ability, we can no longer so easily "forget" that: (1) what is occurring *between* us is in some way a reflection of something going on *within* each of us; and (2) we are equally responsible for this situation.

As we gain this capacity to resolve conflicts through seeing situations from more than one viewpoint simultaneously, we both gain an expanded sense of personal identity. As I am able to see potential conflict situations from "your" perspective as well as "mine," I come to accept *both* sides as potentially "mine."

From such an attitude I am more able to stop blaming and start supporting. I can now more easily *forgive* you for not being ideal. We can begin to *teach* each other how to be. We can accept what is, understand how it came to be, stop blaming ourselves, and take constructive action toward *changing* it.

Everything I ever wanted
  but was afraid to ask for
    you can give me
      if I show you how

Want to try?

Don't be afraid
that I won't like it.

Assume that it won't be perfect
for me
because you're not me

Only I know how I like it best
And it's up to me to show you:
with positive feedback — "that's the way I like it"
with negative feedback — "I want more (or less) of that"

Sounds simple, doesn't it?
But we know better —
We know how well we've determined
the type of feedback we get,
how good we are at controlling our environment
to conform to what we think we need

So how can we ever trust
another person to be a real and separate other
beyond our control
  and yet open to us?

Do we know our Selves well enough
  to let go of our egos?
  (the road to Love is paved with fractured egos.)

I feel weak
and somewhat ill-prepared for this journey
But I have tremendous determination
because I know what I want

I want to open myself to you
so we can see and feel each other
  and recognize
    our Identity

It'll take a long time
  but since there's nothing else to do,
    Let's do it.

Stabilizing the Power Struggle Within

Through the self-and-other-awareness work accomplished by such methods as the ones described here, each person recognizes that *individual* blocks to intimacy, rather than resistances to the *partner* as a person, can be responsible for apparent power conflicts. And once partners stop taking such difficulties *personally*, they can begin to support each other. As they come to understand the power struggle *within* in this way, they understand that filling such "holes in one's wholeness" is a developmental process which takes time. They are less impatient with themselves when they recognize that lack of skill in expressing one's love does not necessarily indicate that the love does not exist.

It is perhaps easier to support one anothers' quest toward wholeness and intimacy when we've seen the habit patterns in operation over some period of time, so that they have become somewhat predictable and less catastrophic. Thus, it is necessary that a certain amount of time be spent in power conflicts before a couple can learn to deal with such conflicts in a way that doesn't threaten to destroy the relationship.

Once we stop *blaming* each other for our conflicts, we become responsible for doing all that's in our power to resolve them. We give up acting as if directed by forces beyond our control when we begin to be aware of how we've let ourselves play victim.

To do this requires the ability to set limits on oneself as well as on one's partner — to carry on the inner struggle to manage conflicting needs and impulses, without automatically projecting this conflict onto one's partner and causing a fight. Thus, when I feel a conflict between "doing my thing" and "doing *our* thing", I see the conflict as within *me*, rather than blaming *you* for "not letting me do what I want." And I must develop an attitude of gentle self-discipline to guide myself toward *staying with* the internal conflict rather than straying off into any number of escapes, such as blaming, overwork, drugs, sexual affairs, and so on. A conscious awareness that "*I am responsible* for resolving my inner conflicts *and I need your help* and encouragement" can go a long way toward transcending needless power struggles.

As in any work or discipline, I will get distracted, make mistakes and lose my way again and again. Sheldon Kopp, in describing psychotherapy as a path, recommends an attitude of compassionate self-discipline, saying, "We must learn to give ourselves permission to blunder, to fail, to make fools of ourselves every day for the rest of our lives. We will do so in any case. Scolding and self-recrimination are no more than further errors. Instead, we turn toward the unconditional self-acceptance of one of India's greatest discoveries: *consciousness as a witness.*"

From a stable, reflective, witnessing frame of mind, we treat our more unruly impulses as if they were a much-loved child, whom an adult was trying to keep walking on a narrow sidewalk. The child is full of energy and keeps running off to the fields on each side to pick flowers, feel the grass, climb a tree. Each time we are aware of the child leaving the path, we say in effect, "Oh, that's how children are. Okay, honey, back to the sidewalk," thus guiding rather than coercing toward responsibility and away from impulsivity.[*]

Such gentle self-discipline is the stabilizing force necessary to maintain any intimate relationship. To face up to the anxiety that such relationships tend to re-stimulate (such as the resurgence of childhood insecurities) requires confidence and strength enough to withstand continual confrontation with the pain remembered from past experiences. And the best way to gain this feeling of strength is to face the struggles, experience their backward pull and refuse to be taken back. Likewise, the tendency to be unnecessarily self-punitive must be resisted.

During the power struggle stage, Carla and Henry were typical of many couples who let themselves be "conned" into playing one another's "negative mother" or "negative father" image. As we learn to differentiate our real selves from such feared images and to refuse to be thrown back into these states, we force the other to re-own his or her projections. To "re-own projections," is to become conscious of a formerly unconscious (or "dis-owned") aspect of one's personality, and to accept responsibility for this attitude or feeling, instead of seeing it as belonging to someone else. By thus facing the conflict *inside*, the individual brings it more into his or her control.

As we have seen, no conflict is purely an individual matter.

---

[*]This attitude is described by Lawrence LeShan in *How to Meditate*. (New York: Bantam, 1974).

Carla's behavior, for example, stemmed from some important "holes" in her own psychological development. But because of her relationship to Henry, with his *own* set of "holes," certain aspects of her inability to assert herself became exaggerated. Through working to show the individual roots as well as the relationship dimensions of the pattern, we were able to understand it more fully, and to elevate it from a "blame game" to a collaborative problem-solving venture.

Hopefully, during the Stability Stage, we develop a kind of non-attached, "third-eye" perspective, which enables us to reflect more objectively on the struggle we have just endured and to return to the path again and again each time we get distracted, lose our way, or want to run away.

From this "fair witness," reflective frame of mind we can be more forgiving of ourselves. We recall the pain of struggle, but it is not *now*. We have learned to give ourselves permission to blunder, to fail, to be other than our romantic vision (which is a good thing since we could not be any other way!)

Since we are no longer so prone to act as if determined by forces beyond our control, we experience ourselves, each other, and the relationship as much more stable and trustworthy. We've faced our "demons" and learned how to control them. We can govern them rather than their governing us.

And if we fail to do so, from time to time, we know also how to forgive and begin again. Tomorrow really is another day. We are not destined to repeat our pasts.

Self vs. Social Image

Another important aspect of the stability stage involves becoming more conscious of the effects of socialization — how we learned to become a "member" of the society. If we are to fully understand any interpersonal conflict, we must look at its individual psychological roots, its roots in the relationship, *and* at the social context in which it exists.

Social customs, while originally created to serve human needs, tend to become self-perpetuating. Social institutions (such as marriage and the church) generally do not readily respond to the unique and changing needs of individual persons in a self-renewing way. Thus, a set of sexual mores and sex role differentiations, for example, that were once functional may have long since outlived their usefulness for most people. But in order to *belong*, to be accepted, we feel we must *conform* to these archaic requirements. And when such conformity causes us pain, because the prescribed behavior is not in accord with our current needs, we suffer silently, blaming ourselves or our partners, rather than risk going against the cultural grain. Thus, we try to cure our neuroses or change marital partners — rather than confronting head on the norms associated with the institution of marriage.

Carla and Henry moved from the power struggle toward peace and stability in part by looking critically at the social context that had reinforced and perpetuated their struggle. The fight between their inner needs and their negative parental images would never have been so intense had not years of societal conditioning undergirded the patterns. Carla's mother's dependence on her husband for validation of her sexuality....Henry's mother's feeling of powerlessness in the world, and use of the power of her sexuality to manipulate her son.....Carla's father's addiction to the work ethic and uneasiness with female sexuality....Henry's father's uncertainty of his adequacy in the role of provider, and his abdication of authority to his wife.

Combine this with the adolescent socialization pattern....typical conformity pressures governing boys' and girls' senses of personal and sexual adequacy...the "Playboy" or "Muscle Beach" images of physical attractiveness...the double standard regarding sexual behavior...the "meat market" mentality of adolescent socializing. It's a wonder men and women aren't battling each other constantly!

As Carla and Henry came to recognize how much of their personal struggle was a collective struggle, widely shared by men and women in our society, they stopped blaming themselves. This lessened tendency to project blame onto the partner enabled them to take *joint* responsibility for their situation.

The power struggle between Carla and Henry dissolved as each came to understand the struggle for wholeness (and against "hole-ness") going on within each of them, reinforced by cultural sex-role expectations. They began to see more clearly how they had been playing out "scripts" written for them by their parents and society. They determined to author their own scripts to reflect their real needs and feelings rather than living by the authority of others.

As a complement to their couples counseling sessions, a couples therapy/consciousness-raising group gave them the opportunity to engage other couples in mutual problem-solving. The format of the group allowed for individual and pair work. Here, they became critically conscious of freedom-limiting sex-roles and other stereotypes, such as agism, racism, classism, and what I call "adultism" — the inordinate cultural value placed on being grown up, serious, goal-oriented as opposed to childlike, playful and spontaneous. Group members explored the roots of their conflicts in the restrictive social fabric as well as in their personalities.

Carla and Henry, along with the other couples in the group, came to understand how the habit patterns that were causing them difficulty stemmed partly from their lifelong socialization into "appropriate" male and female behavior. They grew to see their problems more objectively, forgive themselves more easily, and ask for their partner's support in overcoming these habits. Each of the several couples in the group was aided by this experience to gain perspective on the "battle of the sexes," toward a greater sense of cooperation, shared power,...and stability.

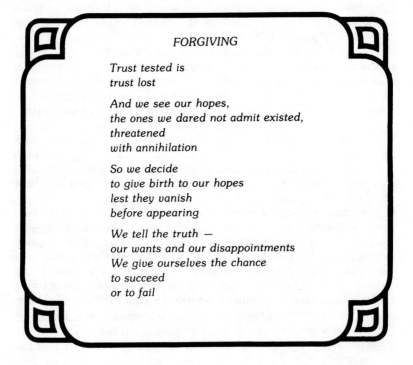

FORGIVING

Trust tested is
trust lost

And we see our hopes,
the ones we dared not admit existed,
threatened
with annihilation

So we decide
to give birth to our hopes
lest they vanish
before appearing

We tell the truth —
our wants and our disappointments
We give ourselves the chance
to succeed
or to fail

The Illusion of Peace

As noted earlier, while the Stability Stage marks an expansion of the couple's awareness and responsibility, it also contains the seeds of an illusion — the illusion of peace.

Couples may feel that once they have a grip on the power struggle, which had formerly been gripping *them*, they have somehow *arrived*. They often feel "reborn" into insight and power over their own lives, now that they understand how to learn from their conflicts rather than identifying with them. As a consequence, each conflict feels less urgent and many may be allowed to go by without attention. The feeling may be "Oh, we've been through this one so many times before...we know what it's about....we can afford to let it pass." And to some extent this is a good way to proceed — unless it becomes a habit rather than a conscious choice. It's important to be able to "let go" of conflicts — but not to *avoid* them compulsively for fear of causing a stir.

Forgiveness is appropriate *after* mutual hurt and anger have been clarified — not as a way of *denying* such feelings. It is the *illusion* of peace, and *not* the stable ebb and flow of close and distant feelings, which cause problems. If we rationalize our conflict-avoidance by a "we're beyond all that" attitude, or give in too easily to each other's demands, simply to keep the peace, then we are caught in "the illusion of peace."

Another pitfall of stability consciousness is the tendency for one or both partners to automatically assume, "this conflict is *within* me...I need not bother my partner about what's bothering me. I'll just take full responsibility for myself...If I'm hurt or angry, it must be *my* problem." Thus, the notion of attending to the power struggle within can be taken too far...so that the partner is shut out of one's inner thoughts, even when they are relevant to the relationship.

True stability is not without conflict or change. Rather it recognizes differentiation or change as the one constant in all of life. Coming to terms with change — letting go of the old, embracing the new, and knowing something about when to do which — is essential for the maintenance of a stable sense of self. which in turn is an absolute prerequisite for commitment to another person.

On page 150, you will find a collection of self-help activities that can be used to further your awareness of Stage III issues.

chapter four

COMMITMENT

(stage IV of the couple's journey)

The Stability Stage has provided the partners with the insight necessary to *understand* their struggles. It has been, in a sense, a period of increased *reflection,* a calm after the power-struggle storm — thus preparing the couple for another type of *action*, for commitment.

Commitment means choice: I decide in favor of *this* rather than *that;* I understand that I can't live forever in-between; that whatever I choose, I am responsible for it working or not working. Commitment means *taking responsibility* for making it work. Instead of imagining how it could be better *if only....* "*If only* s/he would criticize me less... *If only* s/he were sexier... *If only* we had money...''

Commitment begins after the power struggle has ended, after we have wrestled *within ourselves* with the same polarized forces that spawned that struggle, and following a relatively stable phase of living and loving, in which the relationship's inevitable ups and downs of joy and pain, the ebbs and flows of familiar and strange, are accepted rather than combatted. We have thus achieved

OK
I surrender
to the truth
I can no longer hide from
You
The joy I thought would consume
The pain I feared would overwhelm
Me
are present
in us
Now
as they always have been

OK
I surrender

To the feeling "I'll follow you anywhere"
which causes my well-laid plans
for my well-determined future
to pulsate with ambivalence
and therefore, with life
And the truth
that all living things
must die

OK
I surrender
to the hurt I feel
whenever "you don't have time for me"
and to the hurt you feel
when I do things which exclude you
to that awful gut-rending feeling
that we've lost what-we-had
and to the truth
that letting go of what-we-had
allows for the possibility
of what-is.

OK
I surrender

to the absolute pleasure
I receive
from your touch, your look, your smell
from watching you move
from hearing you speak my name
to the pleasure of belonging [which is new]
instead of longing [which I've always known]

OK
I surrender

to the fact that you're not rich
to the fact that your anger sometimes scares me
to the fact that you don't always like me
to the fact that I don't always like you
to the fact that sometimes I think I can't live without you
to the fact that usually I can
to the fact that I'd rather be with you
than anyone else I know or can imagine

to the fact that you stimulate me to give more,
put out more, be more than is comfortable for me —
to expand myself beyond my accustomed limits,
keeping me in constant touch with
the reality of my limitations, my possibilities,
and my responsibilities

OK
I surrender
to this demanding, challenging, disappointing, imperfect,
painful, blissful, unpredictable
life.

commitment, a stable-yet-flowing sense of ourselves-in-relationship.

Commitment becomes possible when we stop trying to change things (ourselves as well as our partners) to conform to our preconceived expectations. When we surrender to *what is*. Commitment is, in a sense, a "letting go"...letting go of our attachment to "the way it's supposed to be" (which often meant "painless"); ...letting go of the fantasy that we can win the power struggle, or remain unchangingly "together"; ...letting go of the need to be "on top", to save face, to protect our egos, to have our own way, to hang on to what we've got.

Commitment accepts the rhythms of change — the changing needs for closeness vs. distance, for example — between two people. It assumes that the partner is basically trustworthy and will not perceive *differences* as *threats*, or *changes* as *losses*. This sense of trust has been earned through the confrontation of many differences (during the Power Struggle Stage) and many changes (during the Stability Stage)

The Goal of Commitment

The goal of the Commitment Stage is for each person to feel "I can be fully myself in this relationship. I can express my own deepest truth and still be supportive of my partner's self-expression. I can dare to be honest without fear of punishment or blame. We can support the development of each other's inner essence, even if this doesn't always please our self-centered egos, since we realize that it is our individual essences that form the basis for our bond to one another." We are able to do all this because of our sense that: "whatever happens, we will not be victims of circumstance; we will act on our environment rather than passively reacting; we will take responsibility for creating our reality!"

We learned to share power in the Stability Stage. We now also learn how to *consciously choose* when to do what in the service of our aim: when to act assertively and when to yield; when to be serious and when to play; when to tell the "whole truth" and when to be selective in our expressions. *Consciousness* and *choice* are prerequisites to a committed relationship. We are aware of the fact of choosing in *every* living minute. We understand that whatever events life offers to us, we have a choice in how we respond. We can accept or reject what is offered. We can cooperate or resist. We can see it as a problem or an opportunity. Thus, we have taken the flexibility of perspective gained in the reflective Stability Stage and embellished it with an ability not only to *see* things in alternative ways, but to actually *create* alternative outcomes for ourselves.

Commitment means the ability to act with intention. In order to do this, we must be able to understand certain principles of "how things happen," and "how things are related and influence each other." These principles are learned from our experiences during the first three stages of the Couple's Journey: I have learned that although I may still have strong individual preferences, I can no longer identify too rigidly with only one viewpoint. I have learned that I am capable of more than one way of feeling and that I can often change my attitude at will if I so choose, depending on my aim. I have taken charge of my own emotions and have thus given up, in a sense, my need to cling to any one position.

This makes it possible for us to see the world from a much broader perspective than "your way" vs. "my way" of doing things. We can actually *experience choosing* our way rather than being reactive to the forces around us (or within us). Our choices will most likely grow from a *relationship* perspective, rather than an *either-or* point of view. Such a perspective includes the way it looks from your viewpoint as well as the way it looks from mine, and seeks an action which will be satisfying from *both* points of view. Negotiated settlements. Collaborative decisions.

The relationship which has reached Commitment has grown beyond win-lose or right-wrong. No one is to *blame* for how things are. Both are responsible. Each needs the others' input and cooperation in order to arrive at a mutually satisfying change.

This is what is meant by the "systems approach" to change. "There is no such thing as *a* change," says Gregory Bateson.* Every change is the result of some other change in another part of the system and sends reverberations throughout, resulting in other changes, which result in still others, and on and on.

Commitment requires that we adopt this systems concept — no blame, just mutual responsibility. We have learned well the lesson of the power struggle. We never won when it was "winning" that we were after. We beat our heads against the wall of our stubborn

---

*Gregory Bateson, presentation at Esalen Institute, Big Sur, California, January, 1975. "Unity" and "interdependence" are other terms which help to describe the "systems approach".

selfishness once too often, and came away dizzy. When our heads cleared, we saw the struggle as our own *inner* battle. We needed each other's help in this struggle, and the wall between us was gone.

We decided. We found the power within "us" to *create*. And the power among "us" to *collaborate*. The power to generate *new* ideas and ways of doing things — *our* way — from a synthesis of yours and mine. The creation of such a "we-system" became the only way to keep the relationship alive. Aliveness and creativity became our primary goals.

This commitment — this state of mind and being — requires a willingness to take responsibility, to get involved, in whatever situation we are in (rather than always seeking the perfect situation).

Such commitment can begin only when the search for security, guarantees, and perfection has ended. We now discover a resurgence of positive energy, a will to go forward into the unknown in spite of the fact that it may bring pain as well as pleasure.

Commitment is a decision to *live forward* in spite of our sometimes selfish, deceptive, spiteful, cowardly behavior. With newly-found compassion, we can forgive ourselves these human failings and begin again and again whenever we need to. Paradoxically, acceptance of our imperfections makes possible the commitment to overcome them. If we are unable to face these weaknesses in ourselves, we will remain uncommitted, unable to move in one clear direction (for fear of finding out who we really are?), destined to repeat the past over and over.

Living with the same person over an extended period requires each of us to face our humanness. We cannot "go out and come in again" to a totally "fresh start" every time we disappoint ourselves or our partner. We learn to *live with* our mistakes, to accept ourselves in spite of them, and to allow for the possibility of learning from experience.

Running from one place, job, or relationship to another can be an attempt to run from ourselves, to avoid facing our imperfections, to hold off depression by continually pursuing "romance" or newness from without rather than from within.

Staying in one place or relationship requires that we face — and *be seen with* — our downs as well as our ups, our dark sides as well as our bright sides. "You can run, but you can't hide," as the saying goes.

The map, however, is not the territory. These *concepts* of a committed relationship do not always do justice to what it *feels* like. Although we may be committed in the larger sense, at any particular *moment* we may feel doubt, uncertainty, or fear. We're on this roller coaster 'till the end of the ride, and we intend to stay on it, but that doesn't mean we don't experience the ups and downs in ways that often make us feel like getting off!

Over the course of the Couple's Journey, there has come to be a certain familiarity, a certain stability, a kind of trust that "this too shall pass." And so we know that each problem contains its own solution, and each solution its own problem. We are no longer alarmed or threatened when "what we had" changes to something new. Quoting again from Dora's journal:

"Hank and I are on the 'threshold of commitment', the brink of choice, the edge of knowledge. We're not sure what we may be getting into. We look for signs to tell us whether or not we should 'do it' — when we have only a vague idea of what 'it' really is. Our unconscious knows. But are we ready to make ourselves conscious of what we already know?"

Polarities, Dilemmas, and Paradoxes

Perhaps most interesting among the things I have learned about commitment from my clients and research participants is that the commitment process requires coming to terms with some of life's "insoluble polarities" or paradoxes.

The word "paradox" represents an apparent contradiction: two seemingly polar opposites, upon further examination, turn out to be inseparable and complementary parts of a whole. What at first seems to present a conflict for the couple, such as the polar tension between freedom and security, comes to be experienced as a *both-and* rather than an *either-or* situation. This mysterious transformation occurs when we are able to step back from any *apparent* conflict situation, and see it from a higher perspective — a perspective which includes both ends of the polarity and thus reveals to us how the two are related.

As the journey has shown us, when we identify with one end of the continuum, we can't see the whole. As we step back and expand our vision, however, our identity and perspective shifts. Obviously, in an up-close, day-to-day relationship, we experience many such "either-you-or-me-baby!" situations. If the lessons of the Couple's Journey are used well, each of us will learn to see how the other, simply by *being other* than oneself, is contributing to the expansion of one's own identity. We are forced time and again to see things from a different viewpoint. And since we are in a sense two parts of one body, it is not possible for one to "win" at the other's expense. We are led to create solutions where both achieve expression and satisfaction.

In a mutually interdependent *we-system,* we are continually confronted with things that at first seemed "other" than ourselves, but which after a time, we learn to accept and even embrace. We learn to use our partnership as a way of overcoming our narrow identities and self-limiting beliefs about ourselves. We learn to hold in our vision both sides (or many sides) of a picture before springing into action. We learn that not every problem has a "solution" in the ordinary sense — that some situations remain simply "insoluble dilemmas," over which we have no control other than our capacity to choose a response. We learn that life is *certainly uncertain* and *clearly ambiguous!* We learn to live with paradox.

Let's look further at the "freedom-security" polarity. Most couples at one time or another find themselves divided on this issue, one perhaps seeking more "freedom" to roam or more distance, the other wishing more "closeness" or "togetherness." Yet those couples who have worked to expand their perspectives on such seemingly polarized issues, generally come away with a greater sense of *wholeness*, both as individuals and as a couple. Couples in my study learned to embrace the "freedom-security" paradox in terms of three polar aspects: *Change vs. Continuity, Staying vs. Straying,* and *Promising vs. Trusting.*

Table Two gives a pictorial representation of these paradoxes and the seemingly polar "opposites" of each. (page 83)

In the upper half of the diagram are those ends of the continua which emphasize the need for *freedom*. Below are the *security*-oriented positions. In the center of the circle is the Balanced Zone, representing the achievement of a balanced blend of both ends. Outside the larger circle is the Extreme Zone — "too far in any one direction." While each end of a pole represents something of value, an even higher value is placed on the *blending* of two polar extremes a synthesis of the contradictions involved.

TABLE II

"POLARITIES AND PARADOXES"

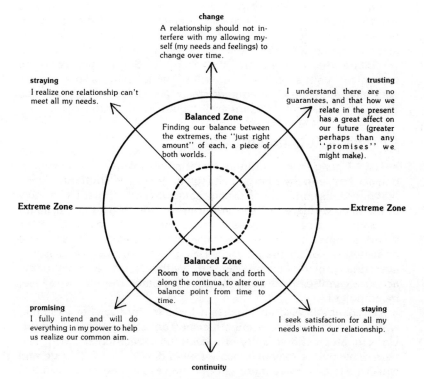

Freedom

change
A relationship should not interfere with my allowing myself (my needs and feelings) to
change over time.

straying
I realize one relationship can't
meet all my needs.

trusting
I understand there are no
guarantees, and that how we
relate in the present
has a great affect on
our future (greater
perhaps than any
''promises'' we
might make).

Balanced Zone
Finding our balance between
the extremes, the "just right
amount" of each, a piece of
both worlds.

Extreme Zone —————————————————— **Extreme Zone**

Balanced Zone
Room to move back and forth
along the continua, to alter our
balance point from time to
time.

promising
I fully intend and will do
everything in my power to help
us realize our common aim.

staying
I seek satisfaction for all my
needs within our relationship.

continuity
It's nice to have a familiar hearth
to come home to — to be with
someone who 'really knows me.'

Security

The couple's work during the earlier stages of the journey has prepared them for achieving such synthesis. Usually, as a couple passes through Stages I - IV, they come closer and closer to the center — the Balanced Zone — although their *exact* balance point does change from time to time (within the room-to-move area). Through continued interaction as a *couple*, they are drawn out of their individually polarized ways of being and perceiving and into more of a "we-system," a blending of their characteristic styles.

Since every relationship needs some of both freedom and security, (or distance and closeness), one member of the pair often becomes somewhat more identified with one end of the continuum, and the partner with the "opposite" end. As time goes by, through continued dialogue during the Stability Stage, we come to recognize "both sides" within each of us, leading us to synthesis and balance in the Commitment stage. Now, "our way" becomes the product of what was formerly "yours" and "mine."

Change vs. Continuity

The "Change vs. Continuity" continuum involves developing a balance between the forces of change and those of stability. I know that my needs and feelings change somewhat over time. I also know that I need a degree of continuity in my life and in my primary relationship. For my actions to have meaning, they must occur within a somewhat stable *context* — in relationship with someone or something other than myself. Being in an intimate relationship over time provides such a context. Without such a context, my actions can seem disjointed and unrelated — in a sense, meaningless.

Yet change is also an important force in my life. For example, while I once tended to avoid criticism from others, I now value it. Unfortunately, the stability of a continuous relationship with one person over time may overlook (or even deny) such a change and cause me to be treated more as I *was* than as I am becoming. In this way, a stable relationship *may* interfere with (or at least slow down) my freedom to change, to risk the unknown. On the other hand, such continuity can provide a framework within which my newer developments can be organized. It can help me test the new against the old to see if the "new I's" which emerge can be integrated within my former identity. It can keep me from rushing impulsively into each new venture without a sense of my history, of what I already know about myself.

Resolving this apparent contradiction obviously requires finding a balance between change and stability, between expanding one's options and staying with what one knows to be satisfying. Each couple finds its own balance, as does each individual. Yet the paradox must be faced by everyone.

Wilson and Detra's "Long Distance Love": In my counseling work with couples I've witnessed some very creative resolutions to this paradox of change and continuity.

Wilson and Detra had been in a traditional monogamous marriage for four years. He had been the provider and she had stayed home, hoping to have a baby, and "postponing" fulfillment of her desire to become trained as a social worker. When children did not "happen" and when Wilson's career as a college mathematics teacher turned out to be a disappointment, they were forced to reconsider their chosen lifestyle. He began to seek ego satisfaction in relationships with other women. She began to get restless in the small college town where they lived, since it offered few diversions for her when Wilson was out with someone else. Yet both of them wanted to maintain their marriage. Even though they felt the need to begin actualizing new aspects of themselves — as symbolized initially in the pursuit of outside relationships — they also valued the comfort, familiarity and acceptance that they had always been able to give one another. They were seeking a mutually-agreed-upon lifestyle where they could maintain their primary commitment to each other, while still allowing some provision for time and space apart. That time apart would afford an opportunity to experiment with parts of themselves that might or might not be ultimately expressable within the relationship. Their resolution to this dilemma was not a once-and-for-all *decision*, but a series of agreements that built on one another in an evolutionary sequence.

Detra decided to pursue graduate study in social work. Wilson realized his days as a college teacher were numbered. Detra was accepted into a graduate school in a large city, three hours driving distance from their present home. Wilson, unsure of what type of work he really wanted to do, decided not to leave his teaching job to move to the city. One of them needed to have an income — if only so they could save up a little nestegg to allow him to eventually quit and develop another line of work.

Detra took an apartment in the city; Wilson stayed in their

apartment in the college town. They saw each other on weekends alternating at "his place" and "hers". As time went on, Detra began to feel competent as a social worker and got much gratification from her work — a big change from her image of herself a year earlier as "sitting home being depressed". Wilson's work life was taking the opposite turn. He was denied tenure at the college, and he was eventually forced to leave his job. He did not feel discouraged by this event. He'd been letting go of his "academic" image of himself for quite some time. Even so, he was now faced squarely with the problem of developing a new work identity.

During all these individual identity changes, Wilson and Detra continued as one another's primary relationship. They felt, however, that they would never have been able to sustain this commitment had they remained as interdependent emotionally and economically as they had been during the first four years of their marriage. Both said that if they'd been living together all the time, Wilson would have felt too responsible as a provider to allow himself to entertain thoughts of quitting college teaching and starting over in a new field. Detra likewise, felt that it was much easier for her to move out of the sit-at-home-housewife role and into the competent professional role when she was in her own apartment and not subject to the expectations engendered by their first four years together.

After two years of maintaining their "weekend marriage," Wilson got a good job in personnel management in the city where Detra was now successful as a professional social worker. They got an apartment together, and at last word they were expecting a baby. Both intended to maintain their careers after the child was born. They expect to "live happily ever after". They do not, however, expect to live forever just as they're living now, for they know that the commitment they have to one another is strong enough to support any lifestyle changes that they may find mutually necessary or desirable.

Staying vs. Straying

The next paradox of the committed relationship, I call staying vs. straying. A primary relationship will meet many of one's emotional and social needs, but rarely should it be expected to meet all of them. Shelia, for example, prefers to be with Frederic over anyone else for most of the things she likes to do. But there's *one* thing which she used to do before they met that she's stopped doing since pairing with him: wilderness camping and mountain climbing. She'd like to start again, but Frederic does not enjoy it. She could try to encourage him, or she could find other companions for camping. In the former case, they expand their relationship but perhaps at the cost of some internal stress and conflict. In the latter case, she meets her need, but it causes her to spend energy *outside* the relationship that she could be putting *into* it. How shall she resolve this conflict?

Usually couples will know enough about one another to know which route to take, and can develop a healthy balance between the inner and the outer. Unfortunately some people *habitually* choose only one option, burdening the relationship with expectations on the one hand, or with possible dissolution on the other.

The Case of Ivan and Yolanda: In their late 40's and married 15 years, Ivan and Yolanda taught me a lot about this paradox. Yolanda, a poet, and Ivan, a carpenter, were very compatible when alone as a couple or with their family of five children. When the occasion required them to interact with other people, conflicts arose. This was the problem they brought to counseling.

We explored together the nature of their relationship, their expectations of each other and their ways of getting these expectations met. Ivan and Yolanda, like many couples who adopt a somewhat traditional lifestyle, found they had no "spaces in their togetherness" (Kahil Gibran, *The Prophet*). When they were together, they were *totally* (and even total-itarian-ly) together. Their "ideal relationship" was one where *everything* was shared — daydreams, momentary ruminations — even their toothbrush! Each had as much access as he or she wanted to the silent thoughts and inner conflicts of the other. There was no private space. No room of one's own.

Once I asked them to take me on an imaginary tour of their home, describing to me the character and function of each room as well as "who this space is for" or "who is responsible for this space". This excursion revealed quite graphically their pattern of shared ownership of everything. Every room they passed through in this fantasy excursion was *common* space — able to be shared at any time by the other without question or negotiation.

It was interesting to note this pattern in contrast with that in *social situations* with other people. With the possibility for relationships which excluded the partner, their togetherness fell apart. In fact they seemed to almost avoid each other in such settings.

I tend to see such "symptoms" in a relationship as messages or communications about what needs are not being met. And *their* "symptom" seemed to be saying — "leave me alone to do my own thing." Yet, verbally and consciously it was difficult for them to own this. (They even shared the same *symptom*!)

As we explored further the "payoff" for this behavior, we discovered that their public — yet silent — protest was simply a request for more separateness, both at home and in social settings. Their relationship was carrying too heavy a load. There really were parts of each of them — interests, pastimes, feelings — that might more satisfyingly be shared with others besides their primary partner.

Over time they began to experiment with more separateness — first in terms of feelings in our sessions and later in terms of activities outside the home. Finally, their whole world became much more clearly differentiated. so that each of them spent some portion of each week together, some time alone, some time with each of the children individually, some time with mutual friends and some time with friends and projects that excluded the other. They spent a long time talking about and rehearsing this last alternative before actually doing it — as a way of reassuring themselves that this change did not mean that they were less committed to or interested in each other.

As often occurs, people who have to struggle to overcome a problem (such as the fear of separateness in this instance), seem to achieve more careful and thorough resolution of it. For a time, Ivan and Yolanda swung from one extreme to the other on the issue, but their willingness to test the limits on both ends of the spectrum gave them confidence in their bond with one another. They were able to see clearly the full range of possibilities between total togetherness and total separateness, allowing them to choose among a wide array of options.

Their resolution to the staying-vs.-straying paradox was to realize that they had several choices at any given moment — some might be more desirable than others, but none was mandatory. Thus, their rigidly compulsive pattern of side-by-side-through-all-kinds-of-weather gave way to a more flexible attitude of side-by-side-at-various-distances, depending upon the needs of the relationship at the time.

Promising vs. Trusting

Our third example is the paradox of *promising vs. trusting*. Once a course of action has been chosen, it can also be un-chosen. I may commit myself fully to something or someone, and I may at any time un-commit myself. The paradox of commitment is that I make a statement of intention to another person, governed by some system of accountability, yet both know either of us can violate the agreement at any time. We trust that we won't, and that trust is the other side of commitment. In order to enter into a committed relationship, we both must have already made peace with the fact that there are no guarantees.

Such a commitment is an act of great courage, and the stakes are high. I might say, for example, "From this moment onward, I intend to be sexually monogamous." This implies that I will do everything in my power to make this a reality. If I fail to meet my commitment, I lose self-respect and trust from others. My life becomes more and more out of my control if I continue to disown responsibility for it. Broken agreements clog the pores of self-responsibility. A pattern of such letdowns may lead to a loss of all sense of personal competence. I come to see others as more and more responsible for me, and give control of my life over to them (majorities, authorities, etc.).

Commitment, in the sense used here, is agreement between two people that they will both do everything in their power to reach a common goal. It does not mean I'll be sexually monogamous for two years (or at all). Or that I'll stay with you 25 years (or 5 years). Or that I'll always love you. Or even that I'll always do right by you. The agreement could be called commitment if both persons agree to share their lives together as a "we system", a partnership wherein I know that what I do or feel always affects what you do or feel (which in turn affects what I do or feel); and I guide my actions with this knowledge. A "we system" thus affords the experience of wholism or unity, promoting an awareness of the interdependence of our actions. It is this unitive consciousness which helps us to live with the paradoxes of commitment.

Thus, I attempt to validate your experience and support your well-being whenever I can without violating my own sense of integrity. I treat you as I would wish to be treated. And if I see you mistreating me, I not only confront you on this, but I also look at my own behavior to see how I've contributed to creating this situation.

Although commitment implies an expectation about the future, it need not involve a promise of the outcome of future behavior. The outcome of one's behavior is a two-way matter and depends partly on how one is received by one's partner. I may agree to let you know whenever I feel out of touch, critical, or threatened in relation to you, or I may agree not to hold any subject of discussion out-of-bounds with you. These are two-way issues. They deal with some back and forth interaction between partners. In contrast, a one-way vow might say something like, "I promise to be sexually loyal to you" or "I vow to stop watching football games on T.V." Here, only one person's behavior is involved — a factor which denies certain interactive realities in relationships.

Here again we confront the paradox between promising and trusting or, said another way, between the future and the here-and-now. The two-way nature of the commitment process, and the interdependence of partners' behavior toward each other, make one-way promises less realistic and less likely to be kept.

When the couple communicates well here and now, their future behavior and state of mind are more likely to take care of themselves. Then there is maximum chance that what they do and think will fit for *both* of them.

To live together in an attitude of commitment requires understanding that there are no ultimate guarantees. The best we can do is to become aware of our real needs and make them known; understand the forces in ourselves, the relationship and society which operate for and against our mutual aim; and *give* to others what we hope to *get*.

This attitude of commitment helps us to remember: we are each responsible for creating our own reality and the world's response to us; the more conscious we are of the historical, social and natural forces operating on and within us, the more responsible we are; and no matter how conscious or powerful or righteous we become, there are no guarantees.

The paradoxes of a committed relationship can only be resolved in an atmosphere of mutual responsibility. When Shelia experienced the "staying vs. straying" paradox, wondering whether to invite Frederic mountain climbing or to go with another friend, what she decided and how she decided it affected their

We live in a world of maya

Hi ya
maya
love ya
see ya

Boys and girls meet greet love and part
daily hourly minute-ly

In the courtship and marriage-go-round
everyone plays their assigned role

Hello
Goodbye
Hello again

Ah, here you are again
new person old script

Couples in search of harmony
find temporary refuge
in one another's crotches

When things get hassled
or boring
we split
or decide to have an affair
or get more involved in our work
or try a new lifestyle
or crusade for a social cause

We rarely look to change
what's between us
within us

We know all about sex
and we've gone as far as we can go with it
we've mastered Masters and Johnson
we've been comforted by Alex Comfort
we're know-it-alls
or do-it-alls
or been-through-it alls

We find that sex can be
a snack
a meal
or a thanksgiving feast

It can nourish
the taste buds
the belly
or the soul

We experience such soul-feasting
rarely
if at all

We love each other
or so we say
but words don't nourish
our deepest hunger
for wholeness

for wholi-ness

Wholiness comes
through recognition
I see in you
what I was only half-faintly-aware-of
in me

knowing once again
what I always knew
as if
for the first time:
re-cognition

Wholiness comes
through touching
your you
with
my me

you're me
with
my you

future "balance point" on this issue. The more she goes elsewhere to meet her needs, the more likely it is that Frederic will go elsewhere when he confronts this issue. This is not necessarily bad, by the way. The important thing to remember is that couples do arrive at such decisions mutually, *even if they don't consciously recognize this fact.* Thus, an awareness of how the mutual influence process works helps the couple own responsibility for their actions and choices, and maximizes the probability of lasting mutual satisfaction. Once they understand the nature of the paradox, they can consciously *choose* their balance point along any continuum.

Welcoming Paradox Into Your Life

Entering the Commitment Stage involves the blending of various seemingly polarized opposites: love-hate; power-vulnerability; stability-change; mutual service-self-service; variety-familiarity; passion-calmness. Each of us longs for that primal feeling of union between such opposites; yet we also know that it is the tension between them, our conflicts and our "failures", which most often lead to growth. This, therefore, is the central paradox facing the couple at Stage IV: the longing for union paired with the knowledge that as soon as such union is attained, our excitement and motivation to continue vanishes, and a new longing for union around a new set of polarities may emerge.

The central task of this stage then, is to create a *structure for managing paradox* — a set of flexible and self-renewing patterns of relating which give each person, if not "the *best* of both worlds", at least a *piece* of both.

For the most part *Nature* provides us with such an ever-changing pattern. If only we could relax and let ourselves be led, we would be afforded the rare and beautiful opportunity of sharing the full range of human experience: love torn by hate, hate modulated by love, passion cooled by calmness, calmness exploded by passion, power undermined by vulnerability, vulnerability undergirded by power. Complete surrender to the ebb and flow of such experiences is rarely possible, however, given the lifestyles of most persons in this culture. Thus, our need is to consciously recreate the opportunity for experiencing "life's insoluble polarities" in ways which do not threaten us too much, but which still keep our energy high, providing just enough *challenge* (or freedom) and just enough *support* (or security).

"Open Marriage" is one attempt to attend to our needs both for stability and for change. The concept means different things to different people.* It is unlikely, of course, that any approach will ever give us all we would hope for. The story of Wilson and Detra, during the long distance cycle of their relationship is one case in point.

Maintaining an Edge of Excitement

There are many possible structures which can be created to maintain such an "edge of excitement"** in a relationship.

In relatively "closed" marriages, for example, I have known couples who deal with the variety-familiarity polarity by deliberately staging new and unusual ways of relating whenever things get too comfortable. One couple I knew would go out separately to the same singles bar, casually make the rounds, and endeavor to eventually get "picked up" by the other. They called this structure, "save the last dance for me."

Another pair proclaim "shadow days" in which some particular generally-neglected aspect of one partner will be given free reign. Perhaps the woman has gotten into a routine of being rather consistently calm and agreeable. In such an instance, they might decide to give her an "angry day" — a whole day of nit-picking and complaining and demanding and bitching about anything and everything that might conceivably rub someone the wrong way.

Or perhaps the husband has been overly involved in the routine of his work to the exclusion of his spouse. A "love day" might be called for in this case. Here, he would allow free reign to his tender, loving, attentive feelings, putting aside for a time all competing demands.

Such "shadow days" can be called for anytime the couple or either partner feels in a rut. If an entire day is not feasible, an hour or two will often suffice to break up an old pattern and point the way toward expanded options.

---

*See O'Neil, N. and O'Neil, G. *Open Marriage*. New York: Avon, 1972.

**The exact balance point of just enough challenge and just enough support can be called the "edge of excitement"; while learning to live at this edge may be called "edge-ucation".

A number of other structures for "opening up" a stale or stuck situation are described in Chapter Eight, the section on self-help activities. Self-renewing structures such as these can help us take charge of our changing needs rather than being victims to them. I find the word *re-creation* extremely descriptive of this process. Through *play*, we experiment, discover, and create for ourselves lifestyles, structures and ways of being together which actually fit our current needs. We write our own scripts, choose our own characters, and direct the action in a way which authentically represents our unique pattern of rhythms, preferences, similarities and differences. We give each other permission to be who we are and to expand who we are — as individuals and as a couple. We therefore, become responsible for our rhythms, preferences, similarities, and differences. We become creators (or re-creators) of our own world.

Creating Liberating Structures

Although love cannot be predicted, controlled, or guaranteed, we can perhaps structure and maintain our relationships so that love will be more likely to grace us. We can, in other words, create *liberating* rather than oppressive *structures* to guide our interactions.

A liberating structure has two essential features: it allows for the expression and satisfaction of both people's needs; and it helps to balance the tension between the two extremes of whatever paradox/polarity the couple is facing. The concept of a liberating structure blends both aspects of the "freedom-security" paradox by stressing the value of both stability (structure) and change (liberation).

In order to create a liberating structure, we must have a way of assessing what we want or need and what we already have going for us. We need to know what we do well together and what we'd like to learn to do. The structure is liberating if it uses what we have to take us where we want to go; if it builds on our strengths and helps us to minimize or overcome our hang ups; and if it is responsive enough to change when our current needs are met and new needs emerge.

Structures (such as "save the last dance...") can be useful in helping us deal creatively with the paradoxes of a committed relationship. They can help us "keep it varied" without going overboard into constant activity; they can help us keep it "juicy and sexy" without getting so caught up in passion that we can't relax or engage in pastimes outside the relationship; they can help us modulate our closeness-distance according to our varying rhythms and changing needs; and they can often help us equalize power in the relationship when this becomes an issue.

The "save the last dance for me" and "shadow day" games are examples of liberating structures. Based on the needs and resources of both partners, they help to balance the tension created by one or more of the paradoxes of commitment.

The Case of Duanne and Sara: A more detailed example of the creation of a liberating structure is seen in the case of Duanne and Sara, a couple who had been together in a primary, mostly monogamous, committed relationship for 3 years when each of them decided to enter individual psychotherapy as part of their professional training in clinical psychology. Sara's sexual attraction for Duanne seemed to lessen as she compared him more and more to her "fatherly and very nurturing" male therapist. During this time she was also beginning to behave in a less accommodating and more assertive manner toward Daunne.

Meanwhile, Duanne was feeling increasingly inadequate to meet Sara's needs — especially her affectional needs. He also found that he was becoming more engrossed in his work than ever before, providing for him both an escape from the demands of the relationship and a much-needed source of external validation.

The distance between them was increasing in spite of their attempts to "work on" their relationship.

When they came to me for couples therapy, we talked first about what each of them was dealing with in their individual therapy sessions to see if this might shed light on their apparent need for increased distance. It became clear that their individual therapy work was helping each of them to take more responsibility for their own lives and to therefore depend less on their partner for the little reassurances or other supports that had once been a major part of their affectional and sexual relationship. During a certain period in their individual work, then, it seemed that each needed to depend on the other less in order to learn greater self-dependence. In order to help make this a liberating event for both people — an *opportunity* for the *individuals*, rather than a *problem* for the *relationship* — we decided to structure this occurrence into their relationship *consciously*. They re-structured their living arrangement so that they would not automatically turn to each other for support whenever they felt the urge. They were thus encouraged to rely on their own resources much of the time, only seeking out the partner when they had already tested and discovered the extent to which they could provide for themselves. In this way they could avoid the resentment which often builds when a person depends on someone else to do for him/her something s/he's not quite sure if s/he can do for him/herself.

Duanne and Sara re-arranged their home so that they would sleep and study in separate rooms for a period of time. This physical separation symbolized and reinforced their new attempts at taking care of themselves in some new ways. It gave them permission to spend more time alone facing their own resources or lack of resources rather than waiting for the partner to "come through" or blaming the partner for "not being there."

Both agreed that *for a time* they wanted to place "learning to stand alone" as a higher priority than "togetherness". And so the structure seemed to fit their needs quite well. Still, however, there was the question of *balancing* their needs for closeness and for distance.

They felt they must acknowledge their decreased companionship and sexual-affectional needs, but they did not want to ignore these entirely. Thus, they began to be very conscious about the time they did choose to spend together, to be absolutely certain that they both *wanted* to be together, rather than just doing so out of habit and proximity. The "separate rooms" arrangement facilitated this type of consciousness, since it helped them break up their habitual pattern of turning to the other for support regardless of their actual wants or needs. As a result, although the *quantity* of time spent together decreased, the *quality* of this time increased. The new structure made them increasingly aware of *choosing* how close or distant they wanted to be, thus giving both alone time and together time greater meaning. They became fully conscious of the tension present in each of them regarding "how close do I want to be at this moment?" And they saw also how a move in either direction by one of them caused a reciprocal move by the other resulting in a new balance point (for a time) in their relationship. Thus, they experienced how they were co-equally responsible, together and as individuals, for balancing or modulating the distance between them.

Balancing Apparent Opposites

The concept of *balance* is extremely important at the Commitment Stage. Taking responsibility for living with paradox involves deciding from moment to moment "at what point on the continuum of stability vs. change (or staying vs. straying, or promising vs. trusting) do I/we want to be? Do I/we feel the need for more security and sameness, or more unpredictability and variety? Are we in agreement about what would benefit our relationship or do we seem to have conflicting needs?"

Achieving a balance that feels right for both partners involves the ability to *negotiate* — either implicitly or explicitly. When done explicitly, negotiation is a process in which partners *express* what we are feeling (how satisfied or frustrated with the present situation), *assess* what each could do to help restore the proper balance, and agree on an equitable *compromise* between our wishes for the best of both worlds and our sometimes conflicting preferences. Such negotiation must be entered into with the spirit of collaboration and willing sacrifice,* with the awareness that in a conflict situation perhaps our separate egos can never have all their wants met, and it is not our *partner* but the nature of *reality* which is "to blame" for this fact.

We learn in time, therefore to value mutually beneficial, collaborative solutions rather than separative ones. Through such enlightened negotiation we experience the fulfillment that occurs when I can discipline my separative self-interest enough to make a *willing* sacrifice — a consciously chosen (and therefore autonomous and self-respecting) concession to your wishes.

This negotiation process recognizes the reality that a holistic or committed relationship is a *both-and* or *win-win* situation. It fosters the recognition that by giving to you, I give to myself as well, since we are interconnected parts of a whole. We thus discover the interdependent, bipolar-yet-holistic, nature of ultimate reality when we internalize this negotiation process; when

---

*Note that the root of the word *sacrifice* is from a Latin word meaning "to make sacred."

EDGE-UCATION

Soft-hard
effect-cause
easy-difficult
being-doing
trust-fear
light-darkness
spirit-matter
God-The Devil

I want them all!
I want the most I can have
at any moment
of both sides
in their right-left balance
I want the freedom and the flexibility to be
softly hard, fearfully trusting, devilishly Godlike
heaven 'n hell yes!
I want to yang your yin
and yin your yang

How can I learn to walk that line
that ever-changing
still point
that edge
between life and death

where creation and destruction blend
in harmonious proportion
The Now
Being
The Center

That's what edge-ucation is all about

Beyond polarities
beyond either-or
beyond separateness
beyond male and female

At the deepest level
male and female
are One
at the deepest level
of being
every male and every female
knows this to be true

And at the deepest level of universal consciousness
men and women seek to re-find
their spirit-matter-soft-hard-light-dark natures
thru union
One
with one another

we realize within ourselves and our relationship the inseparability of my needs and your needs. This demands, of course, that we become willing to experience the constant stream of feedback we are getting from others telling us that the more we support their self-realization, the more they support ours. Thus, what might seem at first to be an unwilling sacrifice or "settling for less" than the ideal, from a higher perspective is seen as a *balancing* or synthesis of your needs and mine toward greater harmony in the whole system.

Finding ways to harmonize opposing forces in any situation is one way to keep life fulfilling and exciting. In balancing on the edge, for example, between your perspective and mine or between any two polar opposites, we must find the *"just right distance"* from each pole to maintain our proper balance. (The analogy of a children's see-saw comes to mind.) When tuned to this just-right balance point, our energy is responsive to subtle, moment-to-moment changes in ourselves and the people and things around us. Our bodies and minds are not tense, not flaccid, but somewhere in-between.* We are operating at peak efficiency with full attention to the moment.

The ability to fully experience oneself at the edge or balance point also enables us to "go all the way" in either direction without fear that we'll lose touch with the other side. This, then, is the essence of commitment — the willingness to go forward in one clear direction, knowing that we can change that direction any time we choose, since we are in constant, subtle communication and are not bound to the past. At the Commitment Stage, the couple learns to live in the present.

On page 152 are suggested some self-help activities designed to help you focus on Stage IV issues.

---

*Some people liken this feeling to the point just before sexual orgasm. Some characterize it as akin to being "poised between life and death." Others see it as a state of consciousness where we are living fully in "the Now," on the edge of time and thus not bound to the past.

chapter five

CO-CREATION

(stage V of the couple's journey)

If the couple's journey is indeed a path toward wholeness, and if we learn well the lessons of this path, what then? What difference will it make in our lives?

Why is it important that we learn to be more aware, responsible, and purposeful? Is there perhaps another aim in our mutual journey, to find some "right relationship," not only with each other, but with the whole of life? Can we begin now to see our lives as meaningful in a larger context, beyond our pair?

Although very few of the couples I worked with were dealing explicitly with such questions, there was much evidence in their stories to suggest that many were headed toward confronting such broader issues. As couples were able to get perspective on their struggles and to recognize the patterns in them, they found themselves becoming more conscious of certain "laws" or "principles" of relationship — principles which could be said to be universally applicable to relationships between any two or more living systems or beings. And as these principles become internalized — part of one's own "inner map" — there seems an increasing tendency to live in harmony with them in *all* one's relationships. Thus, there is a stage of relationship development in which the couple is increasingly able to apply the principles learned in Stages I-IV not only to the relationship with each other but to the larger human community and to the natural universe as well.

Cooperating with "The Forces That Be"

At this stage, the couple accepts responsibility for co-creating its own reality, recognizing that, while some events in our environment are beyond our direct control, our choice as to how we relate to these events virtually creates our life experience. Just as I have learned, for example, that I can meet your accusation with force or yielding, and thereby influence the quality of our subsequent contact, I have learned that such principles apply also beyond the pair relationship. I have begun to understand how I as an individual and we as a couple are mutually influencing and being influenced by forces that we can cooperate with or resist. If we resist, we co-create one set of outcomes. If we cooperate, we co-create other outcomes. And if we are *conscious* of this mutual co-creative potential, we can choose when to cooperate and when to resist, in accord with our values and aims.

Couples who are aware of their co-creative potential and who have come to terms with how they are co-creating their couple relationship, seem to feel a natural urge to create something together — something which manifests their creativity in the world beyond themselves. It is as if they have accumulated a "surplus" of creative potential within their relationship and are now impelled toward expressing this potential, toward making a contribution to the community or the world. The contribution of the co-creative couple might be almost anything: a consciously conceived child; a co-authored book; a mutual artistic expression; a shared community service. The value of such a contribution lies in the blending of the creative potentials of two individuals *and* in the couple's realization of their co-creative relationship with forces beyond themselves. Thus, our creative expression responds both to *our* needs and resources and to the needs and resources of (some aspect of) our environment. We are in this way applying, *beyond* our relationship, the same values and principles we have been applying *within* it.

Co-creation involves two central developments: (1) the ability to choicefully respond to the environment in a way that recognizes our impact on it and its impact on us; and (2) the ability to relate to the world outside with the same sense of mutual responsibility and responsiveness that we share with our partners.

What is "Right Relationship?"

Setting the context for this book in the Introduction, I defined the human quest for meaning as a search for relationship to something outside, beyond or larger than oneself. And in the chapters which followed, I detailed the many struggles and resultant learnings that accompany this quest. The descriptions of Stages I through IV outlined various "principles of relationship" which couples discover on their intimate journeys. But it is not until Stage V that the couple's recognition of these principles becomes fully conscious. It is at this stage that the couple becomes able to cooperate with these higher principles and to apply them consciously in the world.

Here we come to the overarching purpose of the couple's journey: to inform or prepare for participation in a larger world — the world beyond one's narrow sense of self — toward a growing sense of unity with humanity and nature. It is, in other words, a journey toward "right relationship," or love.

Up to this point in the book, I have said relatively little about love. It is obviously an idea and an ideal very difficult to capture in words, probably for the reason that to "capture" love is to obliterate its essence. Thus, I have taken the posture, following my observations and research findings, that love is a state of consciousness, one that we can *prepare for* but never *control*. The couple's journey teaches us more about what love is not than about what love is, since the hidden agenda of the journey is often to *attain* or *get* to a higher, more loving state of relatedness. And through the developmental process of "trying to get there," couples are confronted time and again with their illusions about love. We discover that love is *not* romance. It is *not* power. It is *not* stability. Nor is it commitment.

Having reached the co-creative stage of the journey, we have undergone much preparation for love — for understanding and actualizing the principles of right relationship among all parts of a living whole. We have learned how to *be* in the face of change, uncertainty, and ambiguity — even though we are often unclear about what to *do*. We have learned that we are each unique individuals and that we are also part of a larger whole, where everything I do affects you and everything you do affects me. We have learned also that whatever I do to (or for) anyone else, I am also doing to (or for) myself; and whatever I do to myself, others will feel the repercussions. We are part of an essential unity which becomes clear to us in stages over time.

These personal learnings prepare the couple for conscious participation in the work of the world, toward the creation of a higher quality of life for all. It has become clear at this stage that without such a conscious aim, we often feel buffeted about by forces — in ourselves and in the universe — of which we may be only dimly aware. As we become more conscious of the principles and laws which provide the context for all relationships, we begin to understand that we can choose to participate with these laws toward the ends they seem to be fostering. We can cooperate consciously in the evolution of humanity rather than experiencing ourselves as pawns in the game of life.

Marlene and Michael's Co-creation: A co-creative couple, Marlene and Michael saw themselves as having come together "'to do a piece of work,'" as they expressed it — to create together "something of value" to themselves and to the world.

For the first five years of their relationship, neither of them had been conscious of this fact. "We fell in love and married for all the usual reasons — sexual attraction, promise of a compatible and comfortable lifestyle, a wish to have a family, and all that.

"What we didn't understand until later was that these initial goals were only the beginning of our reason for being together. When little Michael Jr. entered school and we decided not to have any more children, we began to search together for 'what's next? There must be more to life than kids, jobs, and sex!'

"So we began to look inside ourselves for what wanted to be expressed and to look around us to see what the world might possibly need from us.

"Because we were both interested in keeping abreast of all the new developments in holistic health and healing, and because we and many of our friends had done a good bit of research and writing in this field, we decided to start a publishing company that would focus on work in this area.

"We'd both had books published before by established presses, and we also knew some people who had self-published their work, so we knew a bit about the task facing us. But we wanted to do things in a high quality way. That would have to be as important as profits. So we knew it would take effort.

"Our main worry in this regard was not our ability to succeed in the publishing business, but rather what would this cost our relationship? What sacrifices would we have to make in order to do this project together?...We knew also, that this would not be the type of 'togetherness' we'd been accustomed to."

As I questioned Marlene and Michael about their sense of purpose beyond that of enhancing their own relationship, they both agreed that they felt a deep commitment to service in the world. They spoke of the "gift of understanding" they had received as a consequence of working through their power, stability, and commitment issues. And they understood, they said, "that one can remain forever in-between and uncommitted to any particular direction, or one can take action, even not knowing for sure if one's actions will succeed."

"I think the reason we were willing to take risks," offered Marlene, "was because we knew that we could learn from whatever happened. And that we could respond pretty effectively to unexpected events since we weren't overly attached to a particular outcome...And most importantly, we had the strength of our relationship to give us support and inspiration. Our creativity and spirit of shared adventure in the world nourishes everything we do — whether it is related to ourselves, to Michael, Jr., or to the book business."

Thus, Marlene and Michael faced the responsibility for actualizing their individual and dyadic creativity in a way which related also to the needs of the environment. They were usually able to let go of the need to have things turn out a certain way. Yet, they also had a *vision* of their hoped-for destination, a sense of their purpose. Such ability to balance the demands of self and other, dyad and world, vision and reality are crucial to the co-creative capacity. Such balancing and synthesis of complementary poles is perhaps the essence of co-creation: two come together to create a third. All creation seems to partake of this essence. Creation is the integrative, ordering principle in the universe.

The world beyond ourselves
calls

perhaps to tell ourselves

where
we're bound for

or what
we're bound to

or how
we're bound to do

We listen

   to the earth:
   join with me
   in our rebirth

We listen

   to the sky:
   there's more to me
   than meets the eye

We listen

   to the sea:
   when in doubt
   come back to me

We listen

   to our love
   for us
   for all below, above

We listen, wonder, meditate

On what it means to co-create.

Unity in the Universe

This brings us back to the idea of *love*, that elusive concept which is impossible to define or delineate. As the couples journey proceeds, perhaps we come closer to penetrating its mysteries. For example, as the journey progresses, I more fully realize the underlying unity in the universe. Perhaps unity is another word for love. I realize, for example, that as I come to know and accept more of myself, I also become more accepting toward you. I discover that there is really no contradiction between self-love and love for others.

We learn about love and acceptance through coming to know and accept ourselves; and we learn about love for humanity through coming to know and love specific individuals. We enhance our capacity for love (including self-love) through loving another; and we deepen our experience of love for our partner by participating together in a shared creative/productive venture beyond our own intimate pair.

We also learn that love and acceptance are not commodities to be bartered or hoarded. Especially when dealing with power struggle issues, the less I give, the less is available for *me* as well as *you*. I am motivated to develop empathy for you, to see the world from your frame (or frames) of reference as well as my own, so that I can become more able to understand and respond to your needs. This, of course, requires skill, which I discover can be developed only with discipline, concentration, patience, and singleness of purpose. Another lesson!

I have to overcome my ego-centric "what's in it for *me*?" attitude in order to develop the kind of relationship that will ultimately be nurturing for *me* as well as you. Such emergence from subjectivity and narcissism is necessary preparation for co-creation — for extending the boundaries of my identity and my caring beyond our immediate we-system as a couple, to the larger "We" of the world community, and potentially the organic universe.

Fortunately for the coherent development of such a sense of holistic identity, science has recently begun to interpret the physical world of matter and energy in terms consistent with this perspective. The biological conception of *organism*, now a central paradigm in the biological and natural sciences, stresses the unity and interdependence of all life. International politics, too, has begun to reflect this position more and more in light of the recognition that unrest in any part of the world affects all parts of the world. And significant movements are occurring in religion and philosophy toward the integration of Eastern and Western models of reality — toward a more unified and non-dualistic approach to morality. Indeed, the climate of the times fosters a view of the universe as a coherent, interrelated organism.

The couple relationship is a very concrete and immediate context in which to explore this emerging holistic paradigm.

The co-creative couple recognizes a mutual responsibility for overcoming self-limiting cultural beliefs. Regardless of what some "authority" may tell us, we can see now with our own eyes that domination of one person, group or natural resource by another cannot be justified by appeal to God, nature, or even long-range self-interest. For eventually, all attempts at oppression backfire.

The couple's development toward intimacy brings this lesson home time and again. Individually and as a two-person support system, the couple realize their own inner authority and develop the courage to withstand oppression and conformity pressure, both from each other and from the society.

Differences are found to be a source of learning and creativity — in fact, the relationship will not expand unless unmet needs and original (or "deviant") perspectives are expressed and attended. We learn, in the relative safety of the pair relationship, a principle that applies to all levels of human systems: maximum development of the whole (community, world order, natural environment) depends on individuals (or individual sub-systems) having the ability and the support of the system to communicate their unique views, needs, and values, even when these seem at odds with the prevailing norm.

We learn also that the best way to creatively resolve apparent conflicts is to promote in all parties an awareness of and ability to communicate from another perspective higher and more inclusive than their own. Such a perspective includes the view of the "other side(s)" as well as one's own. These important relationship skills — the ability to be assertive without aggression and the ability to see both sides of an argument objectively — are practiced and honed in an intimate relationship, with the ultimate result that they become available to the world beyond the couple.

In turn, if these and other relationship resources (such as the capacity for acceptance and the willingness to expend effort toward a valued goal) are not *used* in the world beyond the couple, they will not long be available to the individuals within it. Here we find another universal law, the *law of atrophy:* ''if you don't use it, you lose it.'' Thus, if couples try to hoard what they have learned within the pair relationship, by refusing to relate to the larger community, they violate the very principle of interconnected wholeness that they are trying to hold on to. And they find that they did not really have it in the first place.

Thus, my "work" in relationship to the world is to express as fully and clearly as possible the unique perspectives, learnings, and experiences I have acquired on the path of life — to tell my story as my individual contribution to human history. Likewise, as a couple, our participation in the whole of life involves our expressing as fully and clearly as we can our unique views and experiences. As we most fully share with others our uniqueness, recognizing our common humanity and shared destiny, we become most fully and wholly human.

The couple's journey can provide us with an internalized map of the possibility of such differentiated relationship among all beings on the planet. It can lead us from "me-first consciousness" to "I-consciousness" to "we-consciousness" to "We-consciousness" — as our sense of who We are comes to include the whole family of life on earth.

These principles recall the experience of love often found in poetry and literature, where it is likened to a mystical state of union — dissolving self and other, me and you, us and them, linear logic and competitive economics, in the experience of oneness. Yet, this state — so potentially beneficial for the evolution of higher consciousness and more inclusive identity — cannot be directed, controlled, or legislated. All we can do is prepare ourselves and wait to be graced. All we can do is *use what we have* (and not hoard it) and *acknowledge our limitations* (and not deny them). This "taking responsibility," a key developmental issue during the Stability Stage, leads us toward Commitment, where we further develop our ability to act with clarity and intention, where we are *prepared* to love, where "we recognize it if it hits us."

Life as a Creation

Our relationship to the whole thus involves attuning ourselves to its needs — just as we have learned to attune to and intuit our partner's needs — focusing on what we can give over what we will get, and upon how our differences are complementary parts of a whole rather than elements which divide us. This attitude involves seeing our lives as a creation, a work of art which we offer to the earth and its inhabitants — a creation born from the alchemy of our two individualities blending into one. A conscious creation. A cooperative creation. A co-creation manifested via cooperation and consciousness of the whole and our relationship to it.

The lessons acquired during Stages I through IV of the couple's journey can now be more consciously applied beyond the boundaries of our intimacy. We have experienced the "fall from grace" in relationship to our romantic vision of "how it will be" in our relationship (Romance). We have tried to "make it work" via power and manipulation (Power Struggle). We have accepted responsibility for the part of the struggle that is within our capacity to control or manage (Stability). And we have learned to cooperatively create a third force (our "we-system") out of our duality, based on a shared sense of purpose (Commitment).

The fifth stage in our journey utilizes the lessons of the first four stages toward relationship with the larger whole of humanity, nature, or the planet. Couples who have experienced commitment in relationship to each other may come to a feeling of being called upon to share this capacity with others. Such a calling will often entail some degree of sacrifice in terms of time spent in nurturing one another. However, if a balance between self- (couple) and other-nurturance can be maintained, service to the world can bring a renewed sense of meaning to the couple's life. Such sacrifice can truly be an act of "making sacred."

At the co-creative stage, we accept responsibility not just for actualizing our vision of right relatinship to each other — but to the whole of life. And as our struggles to differentiate from our romantic illusions have taught us, such a vision may take considerable work to actualize.

We have also learned in earlier stages of the journey that there are limits in our power to control events outside of ourselves. Thus, our attempts to achieve our ideals must be tempered with a clear understanding of ourselves as participants and co-creators in the evolutionary process. We endeavor to understand our motivations and accept our limitations without losing sight of our vision. We use our ability to live with paradox as an aid in the process. Thus, just as we learned both to make commitments ("promise") and to surrender to the unknown ("trust") as a couple, so also do we temper our goal-oriented action with a receptivity to the forces around us.

As co-creators we come together with others to co-operate and to co-create a vision of human possibilities, a vision which takes into account the needs and uses the resources of an increasing proportion of the whole. More and more parts become integrated into the shared work as more and more we each come to express our own unique resources (the "gifts" life has given us) and our unique sets of needs. In this effort, we grow in love and acceptance of our differentness and in appreciation of our unity. We each have a unique vantage point from which to view reality and we need to understand and synthesize these many perspectives if we are to arrive together at a Reality which transcends separate interests and promotes the well-being of all.

Bringing the Pieces Together

It is as if we are all together embarking on an enormous exploration, but our map has been torn into millions of little pieces. Each of us by ourselves possess one of these tiny pieces of the map. It is therefore up to all of us to cooperate in building the total map by each contributing the piece that we have. When I find a piece that seems to belong with the piece that I have (due to complementary needs and resources, or whatever), I endeavor to match up with this other one. This helps to place my piece in some kind of meaningful context — even though we both know that we together are still only two pieces of a much larger puzzle. Perhaps the attraction that unites two individuals in a couples journey occurs something like this. And once our "belonging together" has been established, we move on to seek out our relationship with others.

As more and more pieces come into relationship with still more pieces, higher levels of shared reality and common destiny are experienced. Stage V couples, having experienced this integration process in their intimacy and having become conscious of this essential evolutionary pattern, are able now to actively foster co-creation as they are also "lived" by it.

Thus, we gain a "wholistic" perspective, recognizing that separative self-interest at any level is based on illusion; that ultimately Reality is being co-created all the time by all of us; that life forms and relationships are continually evolving toward higher and finer levels of differentiation and integration; that we can cooperate in this process or resist it; and that the more we choose to

chapter six

SUMMARY OF THE FIVE-STAGE COUPLE'S JOURNEY MAP

As our relationship evolves, we evolve. As we grow in intimacy, into deeper knowing of each other, we expand our sense of wholeness. Over time we gain an ability to view any piece from the perspective of the whole. While we may encounter momentary conflicts between us or within ourselves as we continue to expand our vision, we notice that we are able to embrace more and more pieces within the boundaries of our point of view.

At each stage along the Couple's Journey, particular pieces of ourselves tend to move onto "center stage." During the romance period, our "optimist," our "visionary," or our "seeker of harmony" may prevail. Later, when power issues emerge more clearly, we may give free reign to our "fighter" or our "negotiator."

As each of these pieces becomes known to us, the boundaries of our relationship, and of our self-concepts as well, expand. We see more and more of the whole picture of "who we are." There becomes more room for our various pieces and a deeper sense of relationship between them, adding to our sense of wholeness.

Attempting to create a safe vehicle for the journey — an accepting and loving relationship — we put our carrier to various "road tests." What can it do? How much shock can it tolerate?

When we have a sense of its stability and road-ability, we travel for longer and longer periods in relative peace, trusting it to provide for us a vehicle for confronting life's challenges and a context for confronting ourselves. The road we travel has many crossroads and by-ways, each offering a new challenge and a new opportunity for bringing our separate interests into some kind of alignment.

As our differences become more and more harmonized, we discover that our relationship can create more and more horsepower! Creativity and potency expands, and we become increasingly attentive to the question of meaning in our lives: "Now that we know what we're *capable* of doing, what's really *worth* doing?" We begin to focus our energies on what brings an inner sense of satisfaction.

At each stage of the journey, the experience of wholeness — of deeper relationship — expands, from self, to partner, to the environment, the community, the world. Concurrent with this growth process, we meet and welcome some new "characters in our drama," watching others fade into the background. We meet some new challenges, feel some new feelings, let go of some illusions.

"The path to enlightenment," say the Buddhists, "is a continuing process of disillusionment." When we can see ourselves continuing to let go of "hopes" and "promises" and instead to expand our vision of *what is*, we will know we are on the path to wholeness.

A map of the journey is not the territory, however. Care is needed in applying these general principles. Consider, for example, the tendency to substitute "knowledge about" for "experience of" the journey. The couples I interviewed were committed to *living an experience*. Some may have found my map a useful aid, but they also viewed the map as a rather imperfect representation of their experience!

No couple goes through every stage, one-two-three-four-five, neatly and smoothly with no hitches. Not every couple begins at Stage I. Indeed, it is even likely that you were not at the Romance Stage when you began this book. Some decide to stay at one of the stages for a very long time because there is a particular issue which they need to learn about more than the others. People who have a considerable need to work out issues of power, for example, may spend most of their lives at this stage. Each couple is unique. And there is no "right way" to do the Couples Journey.

The developmental sequence of events does obviously imply a value on *movement through* the stages. However, nothing can be said about the *time* one should take for such movement. Each couple relationship, just like each individual, has a life cycle of its own. Some move quickly, some more slowly. Some penetrate deeply into one aspect of life. Some move from one aspect to another in order to get a taste of everything. Who can judge what is right for another? It is impossible.

By coming to terms with the limitations of the map, and remembering not to try to "fit" into it (like the round peg in the square hole), one can discover its true utility. It can be seen as the two dimensional overview picture that it is, and used as it is meant to be used: to show where others have traveled in order to help each couple decide where they would like to go; and to show some of the dead-end roads that they may want to avoid. Used in this way, the individual couple is still in the driver's seat.

The Couple's Journey map does reflect an order and patterning of events that are somewhat consistent over many cases, however, even though no one couple will fit it exactly. Thus, *attraction* does generally precede *differentiation*. *Commitment* does generally need to be based on a foundation of attraction, differentiation, and stability. And so on. The general developmental sequence does have some validity for all relationships.

Small daily events, like planning a party or buying a house, often fit this developmental pattern also. In buying a new house, the couple might begin with a "romantic" vision of their "dream house," and move through a series of recurring disappointments as nothing within their pocketbook looks anything like their dream. Settling for what is available, they will work out a stable "relationship" to this house, eventually acknowledging it as their choice, accompanied by a commitment to make the best of it. As they "own" the house more and more, they put more of themselves into it and "create" it as their own. Eventually, they succeed in bringing it closer and closer into alignment with their original vision.

Many such everyday events fall into a similar sequence. Recognition of this process can help us trust and cooperate with the flow rather than trying to swim upstream.

A map of the journey helps us maintain our "sense of the whole" — of how our past, present, and future interrelate, and of how these cycles recur in many dimensions of our lives.

It is also worth noting that *within* each stage, elements of each of the other stages are present. Thus, during *Romance,* we have our less obvious power struggles; as during the *Power Struggle,* romantic feelings often come into play. And, of course, there is a certain type of *commitment* necessary at each stage just to keep us hanging in there! All five dimensions are *potentially* present all the time. What differentiates one stage from another is the fact that one particular issue becomes *most* salient for that period of time. That period will last as long as there is work to be done on that issue. Once some sort of "resolution" is reached — even though it will never be a "complete" or "final" resolution — we move on to the next stage.

As with all developmental processes, there is rarely a distinct point of division between one stage and the next. As we begin to resolve some of our power issues, we are also beginning to develop greater stability; as we become able to act with committed intention, we are also moving toward co-creation. And so forth. Useful as it is, a map is too much like a still snapshot to accurately portray the dynamic movement of the Couple's Journey.

Yet, the map at least names the key elements, helping us to remember the holistic relationship among them. And although our pictures are two-dimensional and our language is linear, this naming process reminds us of deeper truths that cannot be named.

Summing up, then, here are the key principles discovered during the various stages of our journey.

1. The Principle of Continual Emergence: Above all, the Couples Journey is an on-going process without an end. Each problem encountered on the path is resolved once we have the courage to face it. Yet each resolution brings us to the next stage where new, subtler and deeper issues arise. We are always in a process of *becoming more whole.* We are continually emerging and being re-born.

2. The Principle of Developmental Progression: Certain kinds of learnings tend to follow from or build upon others, creating a somewhat orderly — yet changeable — progression.

3. The Principle of Co-Equality: Before we can act as a unit, there needs to be ample opportunity for all voices to be heard — the voices of our various internal "characters" as well as the voices of both members of the couple. The unique contribution of each person must be valued equally. And each must give or take equal responsibility if a joint product is to be created.

4. The Principle of Giving in Order to Receive: When we respect each other's uniqueness and individuality, we are both more able to *give* ourselves to the relationship. And in so doing, we find that we don't *give up* ourselves but instead, through giving, become more rather than less. Rather than losing what is essentially mine, I gain by its exposure and confrontation.

'If we can lose ourselves, we can gain the whole world."

5. The Principle of Complementarity: The broader lesson of the Couple's Journey is not how to make men and women alike, but how to benefit from their essential differences — how to bring about an emergence which gains from these very differences. Thus, we are together and need each other just *because* we each hold a unique, one-and-only piece of the whole puzzle. We are learning, then, that since no one can be all or know all, we must begin to "form wholes," to create together a holistic universe that has a sense of its various interdependent parts.

6. The Principle of Respect for Differences: We have found that it really is safe to be different — that differences in needs and perspectives are not necessarily life-threatening. We don't have to pretend to be "normal." And besides, the only way a new being can be created is by bringing together two different living beings. The more we allow our individuality to flourish, the more we have to offer in the creation of a joint product.

7. The Principle of Mutual Creation: "Reality" is interpersonally created. I can "create" you as "worth listening to" or "boring" simply by what kind of attention I give you. Conversely, I can "create" myself as either boring or interesting to you according to the quality of attention I give myself.

8. The Principle of Individuality: We each are alone in a sense, each with a different set of life experiences and lessons to be learned. What's true for one person may not be true for another. Sometimes, the closer we get, the more fully we recognize this "aloneness."

9. The Principle of Interdependence: At another level, we are all part of one interdependent human and planetary body. We know there are others on this adventure with us, whose presences, as witnesses, guides, and companions, illuminate our path and help us see our own way more clearly. The journey, when shared, is all the more immediate and real.

10. The Principle of Imperfection: We realize that although we never know exactly where the road is taking us, we must travel it nevertheless. We must act on what we do know, even though we never know enough. We seek to attain our vision of "right relationship," yet we know that we may never reach perfection, for we are on a journey without end. As has been wisely said, "life is a journey, not a destination."

We learn to be in a couple relationship by being fully present in our relationship to ourselves. We learn to be in harmonious relationship to a family or larger community by being fully present in our relationship to one special other person. And so on. As life continues, we continue to expand the boundaries of our identities. Love graces us occasionally in this process — perhaps during the periods just before we're ready to embark on a new level of the search.

There are no easy answers and yet, no lasting problems. Whatever perplexes me today may emerge tomorrow into clarity and dissolve the next day into oblivion. The developmental changes that are the only constant on the journey teach me that I must trust my here-and-now responses and act on them if I am to learn what to trust and what not to trust. Paradoxical thinking, to be sure; but we learn that Reality is paradoxical and that oppositeness is only a category of the human mind.

Thus, we are prepared to live with some measure of clarity in a world of confusion; to stand up for our values while understanding how relative and subjective they are; to open ourselves to love even though we suspect that this, too, shall pass.

chapter seven

CURRENT ISSUES IN THE COUPLE RELATIONSHIP

In analyzing the interviews and case studies conducted for this book, a number of themes and issues recurred which deserve further discussion. Although mentioned briefly elsewhere in the book, they reflect the contemporary scene so significantly, I am devoting this additional space to expand upon them:

The five issues I've chosen for further attention are: *Sexual Exclusiveness, Sex Roles, Sex and Lovemaking, Spiritual Practice,* and *Individual Differences.* These are all areas which deserve additional research; they were not the focus of my study. I hope the following paragraphs will encourage couples and researchers to take a fresh look at these issues.

Sexual Exclusiveness

The question of sexual monogamy/non-monogamy arises at some point in most relationships. Some partners are able to agree easily on the degree to which they want an exclusive contract (excluding other sex partners). Others spend years struggling with this issue. The meaning of the question and the impact of its resolution seem to vary depending upon the developmental stage of the couple. Sexual inclusiveness during the Romance Stage will have different meaning and impact than during the Power Struggle Stage. The meaning and impact would be still different if it occurred during the Stability, Commitment or Co-Creative Stages.

From my observations, couples who start out with an inclusive (open) agreement have difficulty establishing clear boundaries in their relationship. They lack clear agreements about what is and is not expected or permitted in order to be a "member in good standing" in the relationship. Often such people have had a life pattern of "accepting whatever happens." Other individuals may have very specific wants and preferences. An all-accepting attitude may work for the partners for a while, but if it represents a way of avoiding making any sacrifices, it has the effect of diluting the significance of the relationship.

Jack and Shirley's "No Sacrifices" Relationship: With a shared vision that theirs would be a "no-sacrifices" relationship — Jack and Shirley decided that both could independently do exactly as they felt. Since they were strongly attracted to each other, they felt secure in the conviction that the relationship would not be threatened by an occasional outside relationship.

As time went by, this assumption was proven to be true — their outside relationships, in and of themselves, did not seem to pose a threat to their security. Still, something seemed vaguely wrong or incomplete.

Finally, as they began to question their "no-sacrifices" concept, they recognized that they were each on a distinctly self-centered course — that they were willing to be together only when there was no conflict of interests and no expectations or potential disappointments. As Jack put it, "I feel so unnecessary in Shirley's life". And as Shirley expressed her sentiments, "I don't feel 'called upon' to do anything for Jack or for us. If being with Jack was *really* important to me, you'd think I'd give up other things I like in order to be with him — 'sacrifices' I guess you'd call them."

Recognizing the cost of their no-sacrifices ideal, Jack and Shirley examined further their wants regarding the relationship and eventually decided that they did not actually feel "in relationship." Each acknowledged having felt "badly burned" in their former (and recently ended) marriages, and they were not willing to chance being once again trapped in a situation which might require meaningless and costly sacrifice. Thus, recognizing and accepting their caution, they realized also that without sacrifice it is difficult for a bond between people to sustain itself.

It is possible that people like Jack and Shirley, people who feel a need to put personal preferences consistently ahead of relationship requirements, should not undertake the couples journey. For the journey, if it is to lead toward a higher social and spiritual awareness, will always involve some sacrifice. This is not to say, however, that the couples journey is the *only* path to such awareness. Yet it is true that any path one chooses will involve giving up something in order to focus more attentively on the valued person(s) or state of being. Thus, early sexual inclusiveness can be regarded as a metaphor, expressing other things about the relationship — particularly with regard to issues of choice and sacrifice.

When the monogamy/non-monogamy issue arises during the Power Struggle Stage, its meaning may be clouded by other power dynamics in the relationship. Or it may be a way of punishing the partner for not living up to one's expectations (formed during the Romance Stage). Or perhaps it is being introduced as a potential bargaining strategy to be traded (or given up) later on for some favor.

Power issues in relationships are always complex and hard to decipher. For example, the "will to power" often masks the experience and expression of other, usually more tender, feelings. Thus, unravelling a couple's power struggle is a complicated and delicate task. And when an issue as volatile as "sexual fidelity" is involved, we cannot expect immediate clarity or success.

Marianne and Frank's "Mother-Son" Marriage: Though deeply in love and "emotionally hooked" on each other, Marianne and Frank could not live in peace due to their differing stances on the issue of sexual monogamy. He wanted to "play around" (their term), while she wanted him to "come home to her." She would "wait up for him" on the nights he was "out on a date," and when he came back, she would "try to be nurturing" and let him know that even though he had displeased her, she "loved him anyway."

Frank sought over and over to "get her permission" to be with other women, ostensibly for the purpose of "keeping his libido alive and growing" so he would have more to offer to Marianne.

The couple's description of their dilemma had a distinct mother-son flavor. She was the all-sacrificing nurturing mother, while he was the errant-but-loveable son. She felt wronged-but-righteous. He felt young-and-vital-but-guilty. Sex was the stage upon which they chose to play out their incestuous drama.

In couples therapy, they explored this and other dimensions of their struggle. While Frank came to recognize his fear of being overwhelmed and controlled by his mother as a basis for mistrust of women, Marianne came to understand her motivation for playing her role in the script as related to her relationship with her father, whom she had seen as extremely rejecting and unavailable to her.

They each came also to accept that theirs was a "karmic bond" — a mutual attraction carrying certain "fated" consequences and certain inevitable (and very useful) learnings. From this perspective, they were able to see how being born to their particular parents, with the particular pattern of challenges and supports available there, predisposed them toward their choices of marriage partner and work roles, and provided them with a set of life experiences and learnings uniquely their own.

By taking this view on their situation, Marianne and Frank came to accept that each person's life has its advantaged and disadvantaged aspects. Anything experienced as a disadvantage-to-be-overcome must be learned about, understood, and worked at. Thus is created one's unique path in life.

Not all paths lead in the direction of harmony, however; and some couples, while they may have such a karmic bond, and something very important to learn about, may decide that they do not need to stay married. Sometimes a brief confrontation with one's chief personality feature or shortcoming occurs in the relationship, after which the couple needs to separate — so they each may work more deeply on themselves outside of the relationship.

In Frank and Marianne's case, the fear and hurt generated during their recent past were so deep that they both felt they needed some distance from each other. They each needed a chance to work on themselves without being distracted by the accumulated pain and resentment their relationship had accrued. They recognized that as long as they stayed together, their current behavior pattern would only continue to be reinforced, making it very difficult to feel safe enough to explore their inner responses to the marriage. Since each of them felt in themselves the potential for successful intimacy, they decided to end the relationship, at least for the present. Each could then work more consciously as an individual on relationships with the other sex (with the assistance of a trained therapist). Later on, they hoped they might "check each other out" again to see if they had been able to break their current self-defeating patterns.

The sexual issue was a kind of metaphor for other aspects of the relationship as well. It provided a focus for Frank's struggle against being overwhelmed by a woman and Marianne's need to deal with her repressed hurt and anger about being rejected by a man. It also provided both of them with a means for confronting their chief personality limitations, thus indicating the areas where each needed to work in therapy.

A decision in favor of sexual inclusiveness during the Stability Stage of a relationship will have a very different meaning and impact than it might have during an earlier stage. Now the partners are able to accept the inevitability of sacrifice and have devised at least some mechanisms for dealing constructively with conflict. The main tasks of the Stability Stage have to do with the identities and self-concepts of the partners: expanding one's range of behavioral and feeling options, and coming to accept those qualities in oneself which have been "projected" onto others (notably the partner!).

Thus, at this point, including other sex partners in ones life could be a means for contacting aspects of oneself that are either inhibited by or not readily tapped in one's primary relationship.

Sara and Bear's Sexual Experiment: The case of Sara and Bear offers a useful illustration.

Sara was a few years older than Bear and had experienced a wider, more varied sex life before they met. She had been the more outgoing and sexually aggressive partner during most of their ten-year relationship, and Bear got used to depending on her to take the lead in the sexual area.

After a time, however, both felt that a more balanced (or even reversed) role relationship might be desirable. Bear wanted to have the space to initiate sex. Sara wanted to be approached and even "taken" sometimes. And although they enjoyed their current monogamous sexual routine, they also wished to expand their "repertoires." They wanted to experiment with other relationships *consciously* in order to gain experience that would enhance their individual selves and, ultimately, the possibilities within their relationship. They agreed, therefore, to "open" their marriage to include the possibility of other sex partners. Their agreement made clear what was in and out of bounds in this experiment — essential to the maintenance of their primary bond. One such commitment was to "bring home what you learn." Each would "try on" some of the behavior learned with others when making love with each other. This they attempted with humor, compassion and humility, with the goal of helping each other to expand their range of options in bed.

Bear and Sara evaluated their experiment as a "partial success" in terms of its effect on expanding their sexual relationship with each other. But it was successful in another way as well. Both Bear and Sara found that there simply were some people who "naturally" brought out particular aspects of one's being and others who tapped different aspects. With some women Bear felt aggressive. With others, passive. With yet others, some combination of the two. Likewise, for Sara. This realization enabled them to come to terms with the meaning of choice and sacrifice at a profound level: if I choose to be with you — you who are very exciting, but with whom I feel more receptive than active — then I must sacrifice feeling as active as I might with someone else. And even if I am able to "go elsewhere" sometimes to experience a different sexual dynamic, my primary relationship is still with you, and therefore my *primary* experience of myself sexually will be as "more receptive than active." That's how it is. And I've *chosen* it.

Bear and Sara's story of a Stability Stage sexually inclusive relationship suggests how the sexual issue (or any issue) can be used to work on the developmental tasks associated with that stage.

At the Commitment Stage, a couple is dealing further with understanding choice, sacrifice, responsibility and paradox. Perhaps, when these issues are resolved (or in moments when we feel at peace with these issues) we can use the term "love" in its fullest sense.

When two people are searching to know shared love, the question of sexual exclusivity takes on a unique cast. Perhaps they are discovering the inseparability of sex and love, while at the same time recognizing that one need not imply the other — a paradox, to be sure. Or perhaps they are developing a lifelong commitment, while at the same time recognizing that they may choose to be non-monogamous or even celibate for months. In other words, they are committed to a *relationship* but not to any particular *form* of relationship. Thus, the boundaries are clear and strong, but always open to change — another paradox!

At the Co-Creative Stage, the purpose of sex is often seen differently than at other stages. The couple has learned how to be in intimate relationship with one another and are now focusing more and more attention on their relationship as a pair to the world beyond their partnership. Couples who decide to be sexually monogamous, usually do so as a way of maintaining a strong primary bond. Since so much of their time together is spent on shared service or creative projects, it is important to keep a special intimate place in their relationship just for themselves.

For most couples at this stage, the days of sexual experimentation are over. They are generally not enough concerned about sex and related issues of jealousy and security to warrant spending the kind of energy that it would take to maintain a sexually "open" relationship. It is true that a few couples at this stage find the occasional inclusion of other partners important as a way of sharing with others the nourishing love they have created together. Usually, however, couples at this stage choose to be generous with themselves in other, non-sexual ways.

Sex Roles

Socially-conditioned ideas about how men and women are "supposed to" feel and behave are at the root of many of the self-limiting patterns that lead to stagnation in the couple's journey. Part of the purpose of the journey, therefore, is to work together to transcend sterotypical sex-roles — to differentiate as a couple from the social "maya" (or illusion) which dictates what a "real man" is and how a woman is supposed to be.

This is not to imply that everything one has learned about gender-appropriate roles must be exorcised from the psyche. Rather, what I do wish to emphasize is that the socially-conditioned roles need to be brought to awareness so that we can consciously *choose* which roles to give energy and attention and which roles to let go. Some of these sex-typed roles are harmonious with the inner self and some are not. Some fit well into the context of a particular relationship and some do not. And some fit with a couple's needs during one stage of life and do not fit at other stages.

Once we can stand back and look at the various roles we play, we can decide which to develop and which to discard, based on our particular needs and purposes. Thus, we may find that *you* always

"Light the fire, while *I* place the flowers in the vase"* — a stereotypic pattern, perhaps; yet upon seeing this clearly — the origins of the pattern and how it serves us *now* — we can choose to continue it or not, depending upon our current needs and purposes and not because "we've always done it this way."

In the five-stage model of the couple's journey, different stages call forth different needs and purposes. During Stage I, when the need is to form an initial romantic bond, too much differentiation too soon could threaten the formation of such bonding.**

During Stage II, the Power Struggle aids in the increasingly important task of discovering "who we really are and want to be."

During Stage III (Stability), we continue to differentiate — from images and stereotypes — with the added task of taking upon ourselves full responsibility for who we choose to be (rather than focusing on how our partner limits or shapes our self-actualization).

And at Stages IV (Commitment) and V (Co-Creation), we are guided by a more inclusive purpose, which leads us to willingly accept certain roles as long as they fit our shared aim without regard for whether or not they may *appear* to be sex-typed.

Thus, at this point your "lighting the fire while I place the flowers in the vase" may have an entirely different meaning than it did at State I. Here, we are clearly and consciously part of a "we system" in which we recognize that the particular roles we each play are not the only roles we *can* play (since we are continually aware of the potential for "the other side" in ourselves). This non-attached perspective on our roles fosters great flexibility of *attitude* even if our *behavior* appears on the surface to be patterned. It also focuses our attention more on our common *purpose*, on where we're going, than on who's doing which particular function at any given moment.

Sex and Lovemaking

A sexual relationship can foster any of a variety of aims: during the Romance Stage, it can be a way of establishing a sense of security or of feeling that oceanic oneness which has universally

---

*Line from the song *Our House* by Crosby, Stills, Nash, and Young.

**I am not necessarily advocating that partners make no attempt to differentiate themselves from the other's image of them. Rather, I am reflecting on the fact that the need to bond or unite usually outweighs the need to differentiate at Stage I.

been part of the human quest; at the Power Struggle Stage, it can be a way of creating a favorable negotiating position or a way of rewarding or punishing one's partner; at the Stability Stage, a way of contacting the heretofore undeveloped aspects of one's sexuality and a way of giving and receiving comfort and pleasure; at the Commitment Stage, sex is a way of experiencing feelings of harmony and unity with someone who is clearly *other* than oneself; at the Co-creative stage, it can be a way for the couple to more and more sensitively attune to one another and to nourish their ability to serve a purpose beyond the well-being of their partnership.

Any one or any combination of these motives may be operating during a particular sexual encounter, and the more aware and honest a couple can be with each other, the more clearly the prevalent aim can be discovered and shared.

The couples I have worked with and interviewed have shown the full range of motives and feelings regarding their sexual relationship — from security and sensation-seeking to harmony with the universal self. However, the motives which prevailed did not follow the five stage model quite as clearly as my opening paragraph above suggests! There was an overall developmental cycle leading from romantic feelings of undifferentiated oneness toward more subtle and complex feelings of individuals-in-relationship. Yet *within* any stage, couples were able to incorporate aims and feelings characteristic of earlier phases, without these "earlier practices" necessarily dominating their present aims. For example, a couple working mainly on Power issues could still experience Romantic feelings of oneness; or a couple working mainly on Stability issues might still engage in sex-for-power on occasion, or sex for expanding one's potential.

Typically, however, a kind of developmental pattern seemed to occur even with this apparent incorporation of "earlier" aims into "present" ones. ("Earlier" and "present" do not have exact meaning here, since in some respects the lovemaking experience stands outside of time.) The pattern which emerged followed in many respects the five-stage model described earlier.

Sex during the Romance stage of relationships is typified by a strong drive toward "flowing together," glossing over differences, maximizing similarities with respect to sexual preferences. Where differences did occur (e.g. between what one partner wanted to give and the other wanted to receive), these were experienced usually as somewhat threatening to the relationship; and if the couple was unable to ignore such a discrepancy, it often took on exaggerated importance and led immediately into a power struggle.

Although the "pretending" characteristic of this stage can be dangerous in that it fosters illusion at the expense of reality, there is a positive consequence as well: it allows people a chance to "try on" a new and potentially satisfying style of relating sexually. In other words, it encourages one to suspend judgment for a while regarding one's "preferred" sexual style, allowing one the opportunity to break established preferences and perhaps to learn that "how you do it is how I like it even though I've never liked it that way before." Thus, the apparent pretense characteristic of Stage I can be seen as a way of allowing a fresh and new sexual relationship to be born.

Habits and preferences are hard to transcend, however. If a new and mutually-satisfying sexual relationship does not establish itself during Stage I, some sort of *Power Struggle* will ensue. The struggle may look more like a cold war than a heated battle, but nevertheless, a *difference* in wants or preferences is the developmental issue requiring attention. Often the disillusionment occurs as one realizes that "I'm not going to get what I want by just waiting and hoping for my partner to sense what pleases me or turns me on."

Sometimes there is a harshness to this realization — especially if one had very high (and unrealistic) expectations for how this sexual relationship would be or could be or ought to be. In such cases, there may occur a *blaming response:* "You're a cold fish!" or "You can't last long enough!" or a *projecting-responsibility response:* "If only you weren't such a cold fish, I could last longer!" or a *distancing response:* "I can't depend on you to satisfy me — I'll just take care of myself." These statements are typical of the competitive, *me vs. you,* power struggle stance. The bad news is that they can be used to hurt or dominate the partner. The good news is that they at least get some important (and formerly hidden) information out in the open where it can be dealt with. Now, it is up to each partner to make individual wants and preferences known to the other and to *reality test* the fear that "even if s/he did know what I wanted, it wouldn't make any difference." Such reality testing can only lead to greater clarity about the viability of the relationship, thereby leading to its further development or — in some cases — to its ending.

If the relationship grows rather than dies from the differentiation occurring during Stage II, a period of relative *Stability* tends to follow — in the sexual aspect as well as other aspects of the relationship. Now, partners are able to ask for what they want in lovemaking without a demand (implicit or explicit) that the other always "be there" and without taking it personally when he or she isn't. As both partners own their differing needs, rhythms, preferences (and even "fetishes"), they feel permission to experience more and more of their sexual potential.

Men, for example, find that it's okay and even desirable for them to be passive when this is what they feel. Women learn that it's okay to be "selfish" and focus on their own pleasure rather than on pleasing or accommodating their partners. They also learn that they are "responsible for their own sexual satisfaction"—that is, that the sexual relationship *between* oneself and one's partner is a partial reflection of the relationships *within* one's own psyche. Thus, in order to create a harmonious sex life outside, one must do the necessary work to harmonize the Masculine and Feminine within oneself.

The Stability Stage is, therefore, a time for inner work, hopefully with the support of one's partner. This work calls upon each to take a posture of understanding toward the other without being drawn into acting out the inner struggle. (Otherwise, the power struggle would be renewed.) This does not mean that the partner is cold, detached, or unwilling to yield to one's preferences. What is important, however, is that the partners not take away each other's self-responsibility.

A danger during this stage of the sexual relationship is that the couple may become so "adult" about everything that sex loses its juice. If one can never act like a "baby" and just ask to be taken care of (feeling that this would not be "responsible behavior," for example) the sexual juices will very soon dry up. Unfortunately, sometimes it is difficult to maintain playfulness and spontaneity while working to integrate new and discrepant aspects into one's sexual identity. Thus, the man who is just learning that "it's okay to lie back and simply receive" may be a bit inhibited at first about feeling or expressing pleasure and only after this initial stiffness (pardon the pun) wears off, will he be able to let the juices flow freely in this new position.

The Stability Stage then needs to afford a safe and comfortable atmosphere for experimenting with new aspects of one's sexuality, an atmosphere in which it is safe to experiment because the partners no longer expect to be taken care of by each other. Each is free to pursue his or her own growth, knowing that the partner will try to support this even when it is discrepant with that partner's preferences. Although this lofty goal is easier said than achieved, I have found a remarkable number of couples attempting to put it into practice.

Couples at the Commitment and Co-Creative stages were more different from one another in terms of actual sexual practices than were couples at other stages. This finding indicates that Stage IV and V couples are indeed more fully differentiated from cultural norms and expectations regarding "how it's supposed to be done." Thus, while some couples practiced tantric yoga, others enjoyed occasional mock (and playful) "sado-masochistic" rituals. There was delightful variety among different couples in my study!

At a more abstract level, however, a theme was discernable — one which I can best describe by the term "being here-now." Stage IV and V couples seemed able to honor the moment-to-moment, season-to-season rhythms and cycles in their moods and energy levels. They did not engage in lovemaking compulsively or routinely. They treated it as special and at the same time as "nothing special" in that they only did it when they really felt like it, which made it no big deal and yet all-the-more exciting and, therefore, special.

Some couples felt they were making love all the time, with or without being genitally involved. Some underwent periods of celibacy as a consciousness-raising experiment. Some engaged occasionally in group sex with loving friends. Some had fairly conventional sex one to five times per week. Some engaged in sex as a way to contact the "transpersonal other" — the essential self of the other, beyond personality, which was felt to be connected to one's Higher Essence, or God.

For all of these couples, the *process* of communication or communion was more important than any particular goal. Sex was valued only when it could be used consciously to express love or caring or to foster deeper communion. It was not used as a way to release tension or get some other need met vicariously. Thus, a certain amount of developed *will* was present in couples at this stage.

Ability to honestly express feelings is fostered by the sense of commitment shared by these couples. As mentioned earlier, commitment brings with it a sense of trust in one's ability to deal creatively with the unknown future. There is an inner feeling of safety and security which promotes honesty and "being here-now."

Spiritual Practice in the Couple's Journey

> "We meet ourselves time and again in a thousand
> disguises on the path of life."   —Carl Jung

Jung's comment aptly summarizes the spiritual dimension of the couple's journey. We are all teachers for each other. In the intimacy of a love relationship, we come to see our own inner essence more clearly through having it first reflected to us by an "other."

Many of the couples I talked with saw their relationship as a kind of spiritual discipline, as a way of gaining a deeper understanding of life and of themselves.

Nowadays we hear a lot about various "paths to enlightenment" or the "experience of God." The "*Zen*" of *Running*, of *Archery*, and of *Motorcycle Maintenance* are a few recent book titles which come to mind. I recently read a newspaper article about a woman who saw her typing business as a "spiritual practice," as a way of "centering herself in a reality beyond her individual ego." Thus, it seems to be an idea of these times that many of the activities we engage in daily may carry within them lessons regarding the deeper nature of the human spirit.

Couples who conceive of their relationship in this way are interested not so much in comfort and companionship as in attaining a truer and clearer sense of self-in-relationship. Thus, they attempt to create together a context where the deepest and most subtle aspects of themselves can find expression.

"We make it safe for each other to express anything we actually feel since we see conflicts and differences not as something to avoid, but as 'shocks' which we need at times to wake us up to what's occurring." These words are from Leslie, whom I interviewed with her partner Tom.

"The other day Tom came home late for dinner and was barely in the door when he began to tell me about his day at work. I, unfortunately, was not ready to really listen to him, since I was still waiting to hear why he was late, although I didn't realize this consciously. After a time of monologuing about his day, he began to get irritated at my lack of attentiveness. At this point, I 'woke up' to the fact that I had been covering up my own irritation by pretending to listen. I acknowledged this, and thanked him for helping me to see it.''

Leslie and Tom, by placing a higher value on "truth" than on "winning" or "being right," found the way to achieve more and more a *shared* sense of reality. Such truth-telling obviously has a profound effect on what they will choose to share with each other in the future.

According to Jungian theory, the aim of the personal growth journey is to confront and reunite with the opposite-sex aspect of oneself toward the recreation of a whole Self. The partner can represent in part a symbol for one's inner *anima* or *animus* — the inner feminine aspect of every man or masculine aspect of every woman.

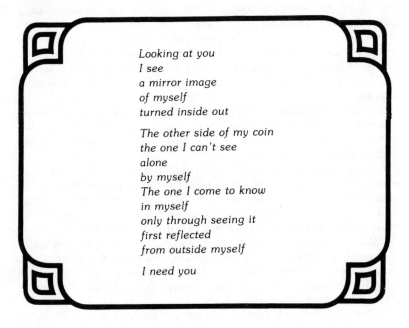

Looking at you
I see
a mirror image
of myself
turned inside out

The other side of my coin
the one I can't see
alone
by myself
The one I come to know
in myself
only through seeing it
first reflected
from outside myself

I need you

As noted in Chapter Three, *projection* is the mechanism through which we first confront our opposite side. This confrontation and the successive "re-owning" of various projections (unconscious parts of ourselves) helps us to expand our identity boundaries toward a more complete picture of who we are.

Thus, male in dialogue with female, female in dialogue with male, experience and come to understand that "other half," and eventually to "own" this as part of the whole self. You'll recall an illustration of this process in the story of Carla and Henry, the two "sleeping beauties" in Chapter Three.

Any relationship, whether it be with plant, animal, human, or our own body, teaches something about the unseen universal laws and rhythms at work in ourselves. The unique thing about an *interpersonal* relationship, however, is that it is reciprocal. It is such a mirror. We touch and are touched — simultaneously. In touching our partners, we experience our own sense of touch as well. Folk guru Stephen Gaskin, spiritual leader of "The Farm" in Summertown, Tennessee, phrases it like this:

"A lot of what being married is about is that your mate is your touch partner, your laboratory, and that's when you can really discover where touch is at and...discover where you're at."*

An up-close, in-touch, I-thou relationship, therefore, is uniquely suited for experiencing the unity of the Life Force flowing throughout nature, man and woman. It's tangible. It's undeniable. And the feedback is immediate. If one partner is gaining at the expense of the other, this imbalance will cause pain or dis-ease for the advantaged as well as the disadvantaged member of the couple. Likewise, when one member does something to enhance the well-being of the other, s/he, too, will be enhanced. The closeness in time and space between intimates can promote this sense of oneness quite dramatically. And it is this sense of oneness or wholeness which is at the core of all spiritual journeys.

Spiritual practice, in the context of the couple's journey, may involve any of a variety of disciplines for harmonizing and attuning one's bodymindspirit, such as meditation, Hatha Yoga, Tai Chi and Tantric Sex. Work, study, devotion and service to others may also contribute, all requiring the focused concentration of one's energy toward a goal beyond one's separate ego.

---

*Quoted from page 172 of *Spiritual Midwifery* by Ina May Gaskin. Summertown, Tennessee: Book Publishing Co., 1978.

While only a few of the couples in this study described themselves to be on an explicitly spiritual path, these few couples shared with me a wealth of experience which did reveal some common themes:

During the *Romance* stage, the sense that "this person has come into my life to teach me something" was a dominant theme, as was the presence of a kind of "vision" of who we are (or have been or will be) together. A sense of humility, reverence, and mystery seemed to characterize the early stage for these couples. As was true of most couples during Stage I, these couples tended to focus on their similarities and on appreciating the positive rather than on searching out discrepancies between one's vision and the reality of the other.

After the "fall from grace," or what we might call the *di-vision,* these couples felt pain and the pull of hurt and angry feelings just as did other couples. Several of these more explicitly spiritually-oriented couples, however, seemed to have devised ways of working out conflicts which helped them to respond less *personally* to the pain.

Margaret and Michael would "stop the world" through a mutual meditation whenever they found themselves beginning to engage in a *Power Struggle.* Frederic and Gretchen practiced a "dis-identification" exercise* together daily, differentiating themselves from any particular role in the relationship and from their potential attachment to having the relationship take a particular form designed to satisfy their ego needs (such as the need to look like "the perfect couple.") Dis-identification is a process of separating oneself from everyday roles and personality traits. For example, to disidentify from one's image as an "exciting lover," one might hold in mind the thought: "I *enjoy* lovemaking, but *that is not me.* That is not who I essentially am. If I were never able to make love again, I would still be me. I would still exist."

As Jim and Anita phrased it, the ability to take a step back from our expectations and habits through such activities as these, "takes the worry out of being close!"

The *Stability* Stage is when most couples (whether on an explicitly spiritual path or not) begin to use their journey for self-realization and consciousness-expansion. For couples already

*See Roberto Assagioli's *Psychosynthesis*, New York: Hobbs, Dorman, and Co., 1965.

familiar with spiritual development practices, this stage seems to progress in a more orderly and even organized manner, since this is a type of work they consciously value and choose. The re-owning of projected aspects of one's being is what the work is about — aspects which are negative as well as positive — but with an awareness of choice about which sub-personalities (or aspects) one will give energy.

Sometimes when beginning to confront unknown and difficult-to-integrate aspects of oneself, it is helpful to build additional inner capacity or "structure" through the use of some bodymind discipline such as yoga, jogging, tai chi, aikido, self-hypnosis, meditation, guided imagery, or affirmation. This affords the developing individual the additional self-support needed to carry on potentially energy-consuming work.

JoAnne and Robert, when they found themselves at an impasse regarding a certain interpersonal conflict, decided to take a rest from the confrontation to allow each to connect with inner resources by Hatha Yoga practice. This practice enhanced their ability to deal with the emotionally-charged situation, thus lessening their fear of the unknown and enhancing their willingness to risk confrontation again.

The re-owning of projections often requires the death of old patterns. Couples on a spiritual path together have likened the developmental change process to the death and re-birth cycles present throughout nature. The process of continually breaking free of old habit patterns by integrating new aspects of one's humaness is akin to the continual unfoldment of life — always changing, expanding, transcending the old, and incorporating the new.

Understanding this cyclic nature of evolution allows the couple to accept more calmly the inevitable transitions from one stage to the next, thus allowing a spirit of peace and stability to influence subsequent developments.

Once a couple's sense of willing participation in the evolutionary process has been awakened, their energy-action will be continually examined for its resonance and alignment with the natural order of things. The development of their "we system" and the re-owning of the opposite-sex aspects of themselves, have brought a sense of what harmony and wholeness really mean. They have become a kind of microcosms, attuned to an internal "map" of how the universe works. In a sense, they *become* such a map, enabling them to show others the way.

Since *Commitment* involves the ability to act with intention and faith in the moment, exercises which help a couple "image" and thereby "create" their visions and ideals are useful at this stage. Some couples use shared affirmations and visualizations to help them develop the kind of relationships they want to have to each other and to the world. Such exercises show the couple that they need not get stuck in apparent contradictions or polarities, that they can use their creative powers to think about and feel what they want to think about and feel — that they are not *controlled by* external forces, but rather that they can *participate with* these forces.

Once the couple feels *identified with* — rather than *alienated from* — the natural order, the creative drive to participate more and more fully in humanity's shared destiny emerges.

Co-creative couples, during earlier stages of the journey, have become attuned to the ebb and flow of change within their relationship. Over time, a deepening awareness of their participation in the macrocosmos develops as well. They learn that after one achieves a relative harmony among the various parts of oneself, and has likewise developed an expanding relationship with one's partner, one begins to sense "a calling" from some deeper or universal source of meaning. I may begin to "recalibrate my gears" for responding to the needs of a larger we-system — the We-system of humanity/life itself. Thus, my values undergo a shift from "what's good for me" to "what's good for us" to "what's good for the planet."

Moreover, their activities as a couple have reverberating effects throughout the macrocosmos. Their conscious awareness of this enhances the couple's capacity to live as an integral part of this larger We-system.

All of the couples I met who were at the Co-Creative Stage saw themselves on some type of spiritual path — a path to realize and manifest their relatedness with all of life. They had owned responsibility not only for influencing each other, but also for influencing the natural, human, and social orders beyond their partnership. They had come to a sense of participation in the process of human or global evolution. They were seeking to commune with and communicate from a deepening connectedness with "Reality," and to continually expand and renew this feeling both in their own relationship and in the lives of those they touched.

This "calling" to participation in a wholeness beyond the self or the pair, leads the Stage V man and woman to follow socially non-conforming courses of action. They do not feel and behave as they once did because their minds and feelings have become reoriented toward the welfare of humanity and identification with the principles that guide human evolution. Feelings of calmness and absorption in work and love life are the rewards of such consciousness — not easily attained to be sure, but certainly within our capacities!

Individual Differences in Development

Couples may get "stuck" in their mutual journey for any of a number of reasons. One of the most common reasons heard by marriage counselors and divorce attorneys is the problem of the partners' seeming to be at different developmental stages as individuals. One partner may see the "ideal relationship" as offering primarily romance and harmony, the other may place a higher value on expressing differences and learning through conflict. Or one may wish for a life of committed "togetherness," while the other wishes to spend more time in work in the world beyond the pair.

When such differences exist, it is easy to feel discouraged and even hopeless because the very nature of the journey requires compatible aims. When two people are at different stages in their individual journeys, it sometimes seems as if they're living in different worlds!

Some couples are able to overcome such a discrepancy and use it to enrich their mutual journey. Others see the recognition of such a difference as the beginning of the end.

Whether the difference spells enhancement or deterioration of the relationship seems to depend on several things: (1) Is the satisfaction of their mutual aim seriously threatened by the difference? (2) Is there an attitude of one person being more righteous or "higher" than the other? (3) Are one or both attached to staying at their current developmental state as contrasted with a willingness to continue to "go through changes?"

If the couple's mutual aim, their most basic reason for being together, cannot be furthered once a discrepancy in stages is revealed, they will have to discover a new reason for being together or they will have to separate (or live, as do a few stick-it-out-regardless types, very unhappily ever after!). Often the original aim is seen very differently once the partners discover that they do not see things as similarly as they once did.

Bert and Karen's Differing Developmental Needs: After 14 years of marriage, filled with romance, power struggles, and a measure of stability, Bert and Karen recognized that she was interested in "putting their differences under a microscope" (as he put it), while he wanted "a life of comfort and ease." Karen had reached a point in her development as a woman, where she felt the need to question things she'd always taken for granted about her role as a wife and mother. Bert, on the other hand, felt "comfortable with things as they'd always been," and was unwilling to indulge her "penchant for picking." Suddenly it seemed that they no longer wanted the same things. She felt she had begun a serious personal search; while he felt she was simply "going off to do her own thing." What looked to her like "our differing developmental stages," appeared to him as "her attempt to cut loose from the marriage."

It's difficult for one person to undergo a major personal change without posing a threat to the stability of the relationship. This threat can be minimized and used for the growth of both partners if the partner who is changing more noticeably can continue this inner process without letting the other person stand in the way. Otherwise, the "changing one" will simply build up resentment for the other.

Another important factor is whether or not the "changing one" can *honestly* maintain an attitude of humility and compassion toward the other. Karen could have recognized her new emerging consciousness as something of value to herself and thus ultimately of value to the relationship. Perhaps she would not then have felt the need to pull away from Bert in order to fully experience her growth. Likewise, had Bert accepted Karen's need to re-examine her life, without feeling that he "should" be doing likewise, or that she wanted to "cut loose," he would probably have felt much less threatened by her changes. An attitude of mutual support, no matter how much a particular change "seems" to threaten the relationship, will go a long way toward allowing the change to proceed without devastating consequences.

Some changes or differences in developmental needs may be more than the relationship can accommodate, of course. In Karen and Bert's case, for example, not only was there an atmosphere of threat present, there was also Karen's very strongly felt need to be with a partner who could share her enthusiasm for using differences to help deepen each person's self-understanding. Since Bert's self-esteem was truly threatened by the confrontation of differences, it seemed that they no longer shared the same aim they had once shared. Thus, with the help of some trusted friends, they decided after 14 years of marriage to separate.

Is it an "obvious" conclusion that if partners' needs and goals diverge, it is time for a parting of the ways? In the "real world" it is not always this simple. For one thing, there are needs and then there are *needs*. And as the Rolling Stones say, "you can't always get what you want...but you can get what you need." Thus, what I may need in order to feel good, may not be what I need in order to develop. On the other hand, doing what "feels good" may be exactly what I need for my development. It all depends on where I am, where I have been, and where I am going. And since each individual's journey is unique, no two people ever travel at exactly the same rate in exactly the same direction.

A major task of the Couple's Journey is to actualize the mutual growth inherent in these differences. Differences in pacing are inevitable. It's up to each couple to decide the right degree of differentiation for the journey they are attempting to create for themselves.

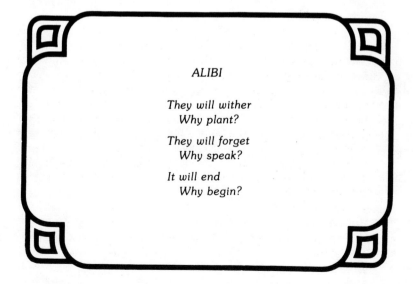

ALIBI

They will wither
Why plant?

They will forget
Why speak?

It will end
Why begin?

The five issues discussed in this chapter — not unlike the five stages of the Couple's Journey — are very much a part of the environment in which couples must function. Yet they are not necessarily "issues" for every couple. They represent important themes *present* in every relationship, but often at a level far beneath daily concerns. I urge you to consider their relevance for your partnership. Have you dealt with each theme? Is it most appropriate to leave one or more for attention at some future time, perhaps at a different stage on your Couple's Journey? Please don't make an "issue" for yourselves where none exists, but do be *honest* with yourself and each other.

chapter eight

SELF-HELP ACTIVITIES
FOR THE COUPLE'S JOURNEY

Refreshments Along the Way

As counselors who attempt to "practice what we preach," my partner and I have some favorite ways to "refresh" our own relationship along the path to wholeness. We enjoy a number of special fun-and-growth-oriented activities in the company of one other couple — trusted and supportive friends who act as "witnesses" or "consultants" to us. Our consultants guide us into an activity and then simply observe us, thereby enhancing our own powers of self-observation. If we get stuck at any time and need help, our consultant-friends simply report to us as objectively and non-evaluatively as possible what they have observed — as if they were a video-tape replay machine. This new and wider perspective on ourselves usually helps get us going again in a constructive direction. After our friends have served as our consultants for a time, we take our turn in guiding them through one or more special activities, such as those described in this chapter.

Couples interested in using these self-help exercises in this way should be sure to read Chapter Nine in Section II, which includes further guidelines for couples helping each other.

143

A word of caution is in order whenever self-help activities are presented in books such as this one: the activities described here are aimed at providing structures for you to see and experience yourselves in some possibly new way. What you do with what you see is obviously your choice. But please do not assume automatically that just because you may not like what you see, that it must necessarily be *changed*. Change is a very elusive concept. Not only is it hard to legislate, it often doesn't even bring greater satisfaction! Compassionate self-observation, however, can lead to deeper understanding and self-acceptance, which then may create the conditions for more holistic rather than piecemeal changes.

The activities which follow are organized according to stages. Exercises aimed at highlighting Stage I (Romance) issues are grouped together; Stage II activities are likewise grouped together, and so on. Although couples can benefit from the activities of any of the stages, it might be interesting to focus especially on the activities for the stage just beyond the one you seem to be operating at most of the time. In order to help you assess your present stage of development as a couple, you might begin with the following self-assessment activity:

First individually and then together as a couple answer the following self-inventory questions:

  a. When do I feel most fulfilled in this relationship?
  b. When do I feel least fulfilled in this relationship?
  c. What do I do and what does my partner do which contributes to such fulfillment and lack of fulfillment?
  d. What would I need to change in my own and my partner's behavior to transform the least fulfilling situations into more fulfilling ones?
  e. What am I learning from the relationship just as it is — without changing anything?

After you have answered these questions, review your answers in order to determine which issues you seem most concerned with right now:

Issues of *romance:* involving a mutual concern with discovering who we are together; articulating our vision; learning to see and hear each other free of "images".

Issues of *power*: involving concern about roles and expectations; recognizing our differences, our feelings about these differences; and our tolerance for differences; access to resources (such as the other's time, space in our house); individual styles of negotiating and influencing.

Issues of *stability:* involving concern with achieving self-responsibility; balancing power and love; balancing variety and familiarity; "re-owning projections".

Issues of *commitment:* involving development of a "we consciousness"; developing our mutual will or ability to act as a unit; living with paradox and uncertainty.

Issues of *co-creation:* involving concerns of mutually creating a shared life; manifesting our plans and visions through creative projects.

Activities for the Romance Stage

In addition to introducing substantive Stage I concerns, these activities also give participants practice using basic communication skills like observing and listening which can serve as a foundation for deeper work.

a. Describing what you see

Partners sit facing each other. Decide who is going to start. The first person takes 5 minutes simply to look at the partner and describe, as concretely as possible exactly what he or she sees, including observable characteristics and behaviors, but trying to avoid all interpretations and evaluations. The second person listens without comment, paying attention to whatever feelings (e.g., self-evaluations or judgements) occur within him or her. After 5 minutes partners reverse roles. Sharing of feelings about how it felt to observe and be observed is best done after both have experienced both positions.

This activity gives people a structure for getting in touch with "here-and-now" perceptions, free of past stereotypes and future fears or expectations. Some of the things they observe in the partner they will be pleased with; other things will be not-so-pleasing. This is the way it is. Waiting until the end of the activity before sharing feelings of pleasure or displeasure can help people let go of their attachment to always being pleasing or always having control over how another person sees oneself; or of the need to always explain, soften, or modify their perceptions for fear of hurting someone's feelings; or of the need to always receive feedback from the other about how one's statements have been received.

b. I see. . . I imagine

The purpose of this Gestalt Therapy exercise is to aid in clarifying the boundary between self and other. Partners sit facing one another. In turn, first one and then the other looks at the partner and makes a statement about what she/he sees (as in "describing what you see" above). This may include the partner's appearance, facial expression, body posture, gestures or other observable behavior. This is the "I see..." part of the statement. After stating what is seen, one then makes an inference or fantasy about what the other person might be experiencing with regard to the observable characteristic just noted. For example, "*I see* you nodding your head" might be followed by, "and *I imagine* you're agreeing with what I just said," would be a *behavioral description* followed by an *inference* **or** fantasy about the other. Another example would be, "I see you with your hand over your mouth. and I imagine you don't want to tell me what you're thinking." A lively exchange of such statements should occur for anywhere from five to fifteen minutes.

As in the first exercise, partners wait until the structured part of the activity is finished before sharing feelings *about* the activity or about how they felt doing this. It often takes quite a bit of self-discipline to refrain from checking one's inferences for "accuracy" and to avoid giving each other feedback regarding the "accuracy" of such inferences. "Sitting with one's feelings" for a time is very useful discipline in helping people to stand on their own perceptions rather than constantly seeking validation from others. (At *another* stage in the relationship, the exercise might well be done with more continuing feedback and perception-checking as, for example, when the partners feel a need to become more sensitized to each other's perceptions and experiences.)

c. Rogers' Listening Exercise

The purpose of this activity — designed by Carl Rogers and also known as "active listening" — is to give partners a new awareness of their ability — and difficulty — in hearing and understanding one another. The couple sits together and decides on a topic for discussion about which both have an interest (and possibly, 'tho not necessarily, about which they may have divergent viewpoints). There is only one basic rule which must be followed: the discussion can only proceed if the listener can repeat back to the talker an acceptable paraphrasing of what the talker has just said. Thus, the discussion will consist of a statement by A followed by a paraphrasing of A's statement by B, followed by feedback from A as to whether this paraphrasing is accurate, followed by additional attempts at understanding by B or by a statement of B's own position (if the paraphrasing has been accomplished to A's satisfaction). After B's statement, A must respond by paraphrasing before going on to a statement of his or her position or response. This activity should be done for at least fifteen minutes. As in the other activities, sharing feelings about the insights or frustrations encountered is best done at the end of the structured time period.

After engaging in this activity, couples are often surprised to learn how little of what the other has said is actually understood. Some people have a tendency to attribute *more agreement* or understanding to one's partner than is actually the case, while other people tend to attribute *more disagreement* or misunderstanding. This exercise helps people recognize the actual degree to which they are in valid communication with each other.

d. Sharing "Withholds"

This is an activity for cleaning up the unfinished business in the relationship, i.e., for expressing any thoughts or feelings which one has been keeping to oneself that might possibly have an impact on the relationship. It is also likely to bring to the surface potential conflict areas for discussion.

Partners sit facing one another. A says to B: "There's something I've been withholding from you." After which B replies, "What is it?" Then, A expresses, as simply as possible, the thought or feeling he or she had been withholding, such as "when you laugh after we've been embracing for a few seconds, I think you're trying to distance yourself from me." Once the withheld feeling has been reported by A, B simply says, "Thank you," without further comment at this time. After both have alternately exchanged several withholds, then it is permissible for them to elaborate, clarify, and give feedback about the things they've shared. Thus, at the end of an agreed period of time, B would have the opportunity to comment on A's statement about "distancing."

If a feeling has been "withheld," it is probably because of its assumed conflict-producing potential. Thus, it is useful to have a clearly defined structure for getting this information out into the open — and one which emphasizes the value of sharing (thus, the "thank you") rather than the danger of having withheld the information in the first place. Thus, "put down" statements such as, "why didn't you tell me that when I did it!" are out-of-bounds in this activity. It is assumed that everyone at some time or another feels the need to withhold feelings from one's partner and has a perfect right to do so.

Activities for the Power Struggle Stage

These activities provide a safe structure for beginning to confront and resolve interpersonal differences or conflicts. They also help promote the norm that conflict can be a useful stimulus to learning and growth in a relationship.

a. The "Paper Exercise"

This activity is done with the assistance of a third-party "consultant." The consultant begins by introducing both partners to a blank piece of 8½ X 11 white paper, saying "this paper is something very valuable to each of you. I want you to look at it carefully and imagine that it is something very important. Now, unfortunately, there is only one piece of paper between the two of you, and each of you wants it. In this activity, although you both want the paper, only one of you can have it. The way we decide who shall receive the paper is as follows: Stand facing one another and each of you hold two corners of the paper with your thumb and forefinger. Just hold it there between the two of you for a few seconds. Keep a good tight grip on your two corners of the paper. Now, when I say to start, you will have up to five minutes to get the paper from the other person — in any way you can, with or without talking. But there's one very major consideration — if the paper is torn or damaged in any way, no one gets to have the paper. . . you both lose, in this case. Do you understand the instructions? Okay, begin."

This activity provides a vivid illustration of the different way the two people deal with a conflict situation, individually and as a couple. Some people use "brute force" and rip the paper away from the partner (often tearing the paper in the process). Some use trickery by distracting the other person and then taking the paper by force. Some use negotiation, attempting to find a solution that pleases both partners somewhat. Others deny that the paper is important to them and give in without a confrontation. Whatever the conflict-management style of the two persons, it will be revealed in this activity — whether they are comfortable or uncomfortable in a potentially competitive situation: whether they take the "authority's" instructions at face value vs. searching together for a more collaborative, win-win rather than win-lose, resolution, and so on.

The discussion which follows the activity can be facilitated by the consultant and might consider any of the following points: Who "won?" How do you each feel? Did the paper represent anything in your relationship? (Something over which there is an implicit struggle, perhaps?) Is your behavior in this exercise typical or atypical of your behavior generally in conflict situations? If you could change anything about your own or your partner's way of dealing with the situation, what would you want to change?

When dealing with questions of "what would you like to change," it is important to emphasize the importance of awareness, acceptance, and understanding as pre-requisites to change. It's a life principle that one cannot force or legislate real change (especially in someone else) in an interpersonal relationship. What is more productive is to observe and communicate about what we see in a way that leads us to accept and understand the situation rather than rushing to "change" in order to please our partners or to conform to an ideal.

b. Your house — a fantasy tour

This exercise gives the couple a new way of looking at the issue of "territoriality." It helps them make explicit the often unconscious or implicit "rules" or norms about how space is to be used in their *house* (or apartment or even separate dwellings), as a metaphor for their *relationship*. It can be facilitated by a third party or not. The instructions are as follows: "Get into a comfortable posture and picture your house as it looks right now, along with any outside grounds or yard which surround it. First, just get an overall view of the house, a general impression. Now, take a fantasy tour of this space. Imagine yourself walking very slowly through it, feeling whatever you experience as you do this. Pay particular attention to the questions, 'To whom does this space belong? Who controls or uses this space most of the time?' Notice what you feel as you ask and answer this question. Give yourselves at least five minutes for your fantasy excursion. And when you have finished, slowly open your eyes and bring your attention back to this room.''

The discussion which follows this fantasy tour will most likely lead to a consideration of such issues as: Do we agree or disagree about who ''owns'' the various part of our house? How do we feel about the way things are? Can we see our house as a metaphor for other aspects of our relationship? What does this tell us about the ''balance of power'' in the relationship? What have we learned from this activity? Have we discovered any patterns or ''rules'' that we would like to change?

(A variation of this activity is to take an actual *physical* tour of your home, dealing with the same issues.)

c. I Spite you by. . .

This activity helps facilitate ''owning up to'' what most people consider to be negative or undesirable behavior patterns (which most of us engage in nevertheless!). It can be done in writing or verbally, or both. It should be done in a non-critical, ''brainstorming'' spirit.

First, one member of the pair and then the other takes three to five minutes to complete the sentence, ''I spite you by..'' in as many ways as he or she can possibly think of. For example, ''I spite you by snoring...I spite you by coming home late...I spite you by wearing that old worn-out housecoat that you hate ... I spite you by being so gracious whenever you criticize me ... etc.''

Generally, it is best not to spend too much time discussing this activity. Instead, try to simply hear and recognize and appreciate each others' and one's own attempts to be straightforward with one another.

Activities for the Stability Stage

These activities, designed to highlight Stage III issues, show couples how to expand their present relationship by experimenting with new behaviors or rituals which can add dimension and increase each person's response-ability in the relationship.

a. King/Queen for a Day

This activity offers a playful way of introducing variety, and possibly some unresolved conflict, back into the relationship.

On a pre-arranged day, one member of the pair is designated "King" or "Queen." It then becomes the role of this person to plan a day, to be shared by the couple, totally centered around the gratification of his or her desires. The King/Queen is to assume that the other is committed to pleasing and gratifying all wishes, where possible. No attempts to "return the kindness" are allowed on this day.

At some later time, the other partner will be designated King or Queen. This should probably not be done on the day immediately following the first round of the activity, however.

b. Incognito

Here is another way of bring variety and playfulness into the relationship.

The couple agree to go out on a "date," acting as if they were each some new person whom the other had never met. They might arrange to meet at a restaurant or other neutral territory, or one might pick the other up at the house. Each would take on a new identity, a new life history, and a new "story", for the occasion. They might decide to dress differently and even to talk differently. At the end of the evening, they would, of course, be faced with the decision of whether or not they would like to "see each other again." At this point, they could share, as honestly as possible, what they liked and didn't like about each other's new identity. Perhaps each would decide to "keep" some of these new characteristics.

c. Telling Dreams

Telling each other about what we dreamt the previous night can be a good way to keep in touch with our "unconscious" and that of the relationship. Simply *telling* the dream, without working on it in any particular way, can be very valuable. Making this into a "breakfast ritual" is one way to start the day with a clearer sense of "where each of us is at."

Activities for the Commitment Stage

These activities give couples a taste of the sense of commitment possible for them when they are able: to see their differences as adding to rather than subtracting from their mutual satisfaction; and to *transcend momentary differences* toward the aim of shared decisions and actions, i.e., toward the experience of unity or wholeness.

a. Position "11"

This is a non-verbal, *mutual massage* activity designed to give pleasure to both partners at once in exactly the same way, allowing the opportunity for *giving and receiving* simultaneously in a way that demonstrates the inseparability of the two. Position "11" involves the sharing of a mutual foot massage — very pleasurable and sensual, but not explicitly sexual.

To accomplish this position, partners lie down on their backs with their heads in opposite directions, so that each can cradle the partner's foot in the hands with the foot resting on the belly or chest.

Once in this position comfortably, partners can relax and enjoy receiving the care the partner is giving to them, while at the same time massaging one of the partner's feet. Do only one foot at a time, and always be sure to give both feet equal treatment. It is best to use two hands on one foot in order to provide maximum tender loving care.

b. Twenty Things We Love to Do

This exercise was adapted from Sid Simon's Values Clarification activity, "Twenty Things I Love to Do." Each of you should number from one to twenty down the side of a piece of paper. Then, as fast as you can, without censoring, and in no particular order list twenty things you love to do with your partner.

Sometimes it helps to think about the four seasons of the year and to list what you love in each season.

After you have listed all twenty, you are ready to "code" your responses.

Place a dollar sign to the left of each item which requires outlay of at least $20 before you could do it.

Place a "P" next to each item which, for you, is more fun if done with other people in addition to your partner. Place an "A" next to the items you prefer to do by yourselves as a couple.

Put a "5" in front of any item that would have been on your list five years ago.

Place asterisks (*) in front of the five items on your list that you personally love to do the very most. Place a plus sign (+) next to those you believe your partner loves most.

Finally, for each item on your list, record the date when you did it last.

Now, share your lists with each other and discuss the similarities and differences between your lists. Together create one list which represents a composite of each of your preferences.

When you have completed the activity, spend some time discussing your responses, discoveries and present feelings.

Activities for the Co-Creative Stage

a. Project Planning

This activity aims at helping the individuals and the couple establish goals and plans by identifying specific projects that can lead them toward their aspirations. Some will be joint projects, while others will be individual. Some will revolve around the couple's relationship; others around work or leisure-time pursuits.

In beginning your project planning, think over the values, needs, resources and goals that you may have clarified earlier (perhaps during the "Twenty Things We Love To Do" activity). Now, try to formulate some projects that will enable you to realize as many as possible of these values and desires. Consider how different aspects of a project can lead you toward different aims, some providing you with a peak experience that you would like to have, others providing you with a chance to learn to do something you would like to learn, and so forth. Instead of thinking of goals with a separate strategy associated with each, try to develop an overall picture of some ways you can satisfy a number of goals within one project.

To assist you in this process, try any or all of the following:

(1) Think of vocational, recreational, or relationship-centered projects to which you are already committed. Consider the aspects of these projects that provide you with opportunities to learn things that you want to learn, that move you toward the peak experiences

you want to have, that allow you to reach the values, goals, and desires that are important to you, and so on. Think about these projects in terms of what you can add to or subtract from them so that they will give you greater fulfillment.

(2) List projects you have in mind to which you have not yet made a commitment. Consider these in terms of those that are likely to be most fulfilling for you. Make some plans for these.

(3) You might also brainstorm together possible projects. Make a list of all ideas that come to you, for yourself, your partner, and for the two of you to do together. Do not evaluate items as you express them. Simply list ideas at first. Once you have completed the brainstorming, then you can begin to evaluate each project in terms of your values and goals and decide which projects will add to your life satisfaction.

b. Mountain Fantasy

This is a guided fantasy activity designed to help couples discover their individual and shared rhythms and paths: Begin by sitting quietly side by side, with your eyes closed. Now, imagine yourselves standing together at the foot of a mountain path. As you start up the gently sloping trail, you feel the warm sun shining down on you...you smell the faint scent of wild flowers...you hear the babbling of a nearby mountain stream. The path is wide enough for you to walk side-by-side holding hands. And as you walk along together, you feel the warmth not only of the sun, but also of each other's touch and of an occasional pause to look into each other's eyes.

As your hike continues, the trail all-of-a-sudden gets narrower and more steeply sloping. No longer is it possible for you to walk side-by-side, hand-in-hand. The path soon becomes more of a climb than a walk, requiring you to use both hands at times to scale the steeper rockier parts...and requiring you at times to ask for help from each other. As the path becomes rockier and steeper, you experience some fear of losing your footing. The stress of the climb threatens to affect your relationship.

After some time of such struggle, you come to a crossroads in the path. Before you are two possible choices: A steep, narrow trail heading straight ahead up towards the top of the mountain; and a more gently sloping path off to your right, which appears to circle round the mountain and arrive at the top after a longer but less strenuous climb.

Together you reflect upon what you have so far experienced together and consider the choice that faces you now. What thoughts, feelings, and questions come to you? Which path do you choose?

Continue now to envision yourselves as you journey up the path of your choice. When, in your mind's eye, you reach the mountain top, what do you feel? And what do you do? Take as much time as you need to complete your fantasy. And when you are finished, open your eyes and bring your attention back to the room you are in.

When both individuals have completed their fantasies, couples may talk with each other about what they visualized and felt during the exercise. Try to focus especially on your similarities in rhythm and pacing or the potential complementarity in your differences.

The activities described in this chapter aim at helping us shed our habitual, automatic ways of being and open up new possibilities. Ultimately, they are designed to foster transformation in the couple *relationship*, not just a change in the behavior or roles of the *individuals* involved. Thus, they require a commitment to a process of *discovery* and *co-creation*, beyond the simple willingness to follow a prescription.

To offer a *prescription*, I would have to have done a full and accurate diagnosis on your situation, thus robbing you of the opportunity to *discover* this yourself. As a consequence of creating your own treatment as you go along, you may be able to avoid the pitfalls of so many of the "self-help technologies" being offered these days. You avoid, for example, getting caught in the "unrealistic expectations-disappointment" cycle: "growth gurus" may paint such a glowing picture of how you will be when you've completed the "treatment" or the "training," that your step-by-step efforts toward self-realization seem feeble in comparison.

I hope you also will avoid the pitfall, so common in medical treatments, of "the cure being worse than the original illness," the issue of the "iatrogenic disease." There is no such thing as a single, uncomplicated change: a change in any system automatically produces *other* changes. You can only guage these if there is some feedback mechanism in the system (or relationship) to let you know if the original change is having the desired effect. Such a feedback mechanism is a built-in element in the activities described in this chapter.

One final common pitfall that I wish to avoid is fostering "look-alike pairs." This often occurs where everyone who has experienced a certain treatment or training method all of a sudden becomes "transformed" into look-alike, talk-alike, think-alike disciples. Although these activities aim at helping us overcome egoism, they do not promote the loss of one's individuality. In fact, I believe that the nurturance of maximum individuality is what makes a relationship really fulfilling and creative. Thus, these activities offer a maximum of *structure* (likened to the container into which something is poured) while allowing also a maximum of *freedom* (to fill the container with your own unique blend). I believe this combination of structure and freedom contributes to the type of *disciplined individuality* so needed in relationships today. It takes courage and discipline to become an individual. It's much easier to follow the herd.

It takes courage and discipline also to embark on any path toward self- and relationship-transformation. We know at the start that we will be plagued by our habits and fears; that the process will inevitably involve pain and that we may never achieve our highest vision. Nevertheless, when we recognize that we are essentially choosing between *transformation* and *stagnation,* our choice takes on greater significance. As we have seen, evolution will continue to occur whether we participate willingly or reluctantly. Our choice now becomes opting for the occasional *acute distress* of "letting go" of familiar ways to make room for something new *vs.* a more continuous *chronic distress* caused by unyielding attachment to the old.

The activities of this Chapter provide a structure for liberating new and potentially creative energies and responses. They can be used as methods for education in how to cooperate more consciously in the evolutionary process...in the Couple's Journey.

BEYOND THE COUPLE'S JOURNEY: THE AGE OF CO-CREATION

"The animals came in two by two
the elephant and the kangaroo…"
Noah's Ark
Salvation as a couple

Salvation as a species
Salvation as individuals

It all depends on two
And inter-depends on two

Two enter the ark of salvation
to spark new creation
transcending alienation
embracing transformation

It always takes two
to create a third

Self and Other
Inner and Outer
Spirit and Flesh
Power and Love
Man and Woman

Opposites attract
and repel
whizzing and whirring
in two-part harmony
or cacophony
as the case may be

But where is the center of this whizzing-whirring
centrifugal-centripetal
yin-yang energy dance?

The primal creative force
which keeps it all together
Creating a still-point-in-the-midst-of-motion
a Dyadic Center?

And how do we come to know
this primal creative force
so that we can become
co-creators
with It?

How can we come to know
Who *We* are?

I'm beginning to know
Who *I* am
But who are *you*
and you, and you?

So many of us here
in here
and out there

How can we ever know
who we are
or how to be

unique yet related
apart yet a part
of a bigger-than-both-of-us Whole

There's room for us all on the Ark
when we understand
our separate but equal, interdependent complementarity

When we real-ize
(by making real)
the underlying Reality
of our oneness
which begins by real-izing our two-ness

The di-vision
sets the context for
the re-vision

One becomes two
and together we enter the Ark
to create a third issue —
our unity
which is our salvation

It takes two
to become one

We are entering
the Age of Relationship

Human understanding has reached
a level of reality awareness
in which we are beginning to see
that the relationships between things
are as important, if not more so,
than the things themselves.

We are also beginning to awaken
to the fact that this world of interconnecting
patterns and relationships
is myriad with subtlety and paradox
that things are not always what they seem
that seemingly polarized forces may actually be
two sides of the same coin

And so it seems to be

with Man and Woman

Nowhere in the universe
is there more vivid illustration
of the paradoxial complementarity of opposites
than in the heat and moisture
of a real-live, up-close
Man-Woman relationship

Here, as Man and Woman
we come to know first-hand
the principles of attraction-repulsion
that promise-threaten
to save-destroy
our world.

The power of love
the love of power
the wisdom to know the difference
and the wisdom to know how to wield these energies
in powerfully loving
and lovingly powerful ways —
these are the lessons we are learning in this Age of Relationship

And our school for learning these lessons
is the Couple Relationship
the School of Everyday Life
Where we are all teachers for each other

Each one teach one.

"We learn best from those we love."
                    —Goethe

Our Man-Woman School is the Noah's Ark
of the Coming Age — some call it the New Age
the Age of Relationship
where two-by-two we are initiated
into the mysteries of life

The mysteries we seek to penetrate
and allow to penetrate into us
just as we seek to know
and be known by our beloved other

And in this quest
this search, this adventure
we come into deeper and more intimate contact
with what we thought to be other than ourselves
with a real-live separate other person close enough
to be continually touching our own real-live separate personhood.

And somehow, with or without conscious intention,
we become transformed
a transcendant entity, larger than both of us,
is created from the alchemy of our interaction

A new understanding is born
an understanding of the true meaning
    of Right Human Relationship
    of the meaning of the pain and struggle which is sometimes
      necessary in the process
    of the experience of being part of something larger than
      oneself
    of the realization that we are unique yet complementary parts
      of a whole
    of the recognition that while our contributions to the
      functioning of the whole are different, they are equally
      valuable
    of the deep and direct experience of our interdependence, not
      only with each other but with all of life.

The Ark of the New Age, the Age of Relationship, will find Noah and his female counterpart at the helm, instead of Noah by himself.

It will be a School for Being as well as for knowing and doing.

It will lay stress on the study and application of the "Laws of Relationship" as discovered in the Couple's Journey and as they apply to the world beyond.

As a couple, the Noahs will provide shared leadership for this voyage, demonstrating for all to witness, the transformational possibilities of these "laws."

Under their tutelage and guidance, we will grow to understand how these laws apply to our efforts at self-transformation as well as to our efforts to participate meaningfully in the transformation of the world.

How "all the world's an ark," made up of pairs — pairs of

seemingly polarized forces within the psyche, pairs of nations struggling for power or territory, pairs of men and women screaming to be heard by each other, to be recognized, and hopefully, to be loved.

Our co-captains, the Noahs, as archetypal Man and Woman living at this time in humanity's evolution, understand that the "Me-generation" is over. Narcissism has run its course. The individual can go only so far in the creative process alone. There is becoming a need for relationship to the Other in order to carry us beyond our accustomed limits and habits and into contact with new possibilities in ourselves. And it is up to more enlightened men and women among us to catalyze the transformation to this post-narcissistic era.

Forming as they do, a Dyadic Center, a center around which seemingly polar forces dance and whir, the archetypal couple, the Noahs, can help us understand the Reality underlying our present sense of chaos and confusion.

They can help us see that there is indeed a light guiding us toward our destination. And that this sense of dis-ease we are experiencing is simply the "fever of transformation." It is the "body of humanity's" natural process of defense against destructive invasion, aimed at restoring harmony in the system.

In essence, they can help us understand the principles of transformation operating in these times. Most especially, they can demonstrate for us how to live in that creative-receptive state of "differentiated relationship," a capacity which will form the basis for our transformation into one humanity.

By their being-together, they will provide us with a model to emulate. And by the social forms which they sponsor, the context will be created for us to become fully engaged in the transformation process ourselves.

What will these new social forms be like? How will we be schooled in the ways of Man-Woman knowledge?

According to the Noahs, we have a rich and exciting future ahead of us. As they have shown us, solving world problems, just like solving personal or communal problems, does not occur in isolation. Problem solving is a collaborative venture, which works best when individuals, groups, and nations are able to reconcile the man-woman forces in their midst. It also works better when we are able to see our differences as essential parts of a larger evolutionary process — as stimuli to help us stretch beyond our accustomed identities and limits.

In the future, we will enter into partnerships with the conscious aim of using our differences as sources of creation rather than conflict. We will practice the transformational principles we have learned on the Couple's Journey — both in love and at work.

Thus, we will be engaging consciously in the co-creative process, using a synthesis of our unique individualities to actualize a common purpose.

SECTION II

FOR
PROFESSIONAL COUNSELORS

This section, composed of chapters Nine and Ten is aimed mainly at couples counselors. Chapter Nine, *"The Couples Therapist as Guide,"* describes my theoretical rationale and a typical case. Chapter Ten, *"The Couples Group Intensive,"* describes how I conduct large group weekend workshops for couples, and the special emphasis I place on helping couples build on-going support systems after the weekend.

Both these chapters can also be quite useful to thoughtful couples wishing to create their own growth experiences. And Chapter Nine can be helpful to couples contemplating couples therapy for themselves. It can be used as a kind of "consumer's guide" to assist in setting goals and expectations, and in making these clear to the therapist.

Just as each individual is unique, so is *every* couple and *every* therapist. Thus, this section is *not* meant to be used like a "cook book." A better use would be to look at the similarities and differences between your own situation and those described here, and to use this as a stimulus for dialogue between partners and between couples and therapists.

chapter nine

THE COUPLES THERAPIST AS GUIDE

Every couple at one time or another experiences the feeling of "stuckness" — a sense of frustration about "how it is," along with an uncertainty about what to do differently. This feeling may persist for just a few hours or for as long as a few years. Whatever the length of time involved, there is often a feeling of being in limbo, of being powerless to change the situation, of being "stuck" in one place.

Feeling stuck (or as some therapists term it, feeling at an "impasse") often occurs when the couple is at a transition point between developmental stages. Perhaps most of the developmental tasks associated with the Romance Stage have been completed, but confronting the potential power struggles within the relationship is a frightening prospect. Or maybe a certain degree of stability has been achieved and commitment "lurks" just around the corner. The periods of time between stages are often characterized by: (1) the feeling of having satisfied one set of needs, which have as a result become less pressing; and (2) a feeling of unrest associated with the emergence of a new set of needs which we don't yet know how to satisfy. Thus, this feeling of limbo, or impasse, may be simply a result of being "in transition" between major life stages.

Yet few couples weather these transitions smoothly. Most of us at one time or another feel the need for some source of "new input" to get things rolling again. One source of new input can come in the form of couple's counseling, where the couple meet individually or as a couple with a third-party "relationship consultant," for a period of time which may be as brief as one or two sessions or as long as one or two years. Here, a structure is available to help the couple identify or develop the resources it needs to solve its own problems. The couples therapist acts as a consultant to the "system," guiding it toward (1) *awareness* of what is presently happening as well as what both partners would like to have happen; (2) understanding and *acceptance* of this situation as perhaps useful for *then* but no longer useful for *now*; (3) taking *responsibility* for what we hope to create; and (4) *choosing* a course of *action* which will more fully satisfy our *current needs*.

Thus, the consultant/guide/therapist helps design experiences for the couple which make more clear or explicit to the partners exactly what is going on. Once our awareness of *what is* gets clear, it's a short step to feeling responsibility and choice in the matter. In other words, clear "definition of the problem" is a big step in arriving at its solution. Thus, the couples counseling process aims at making the implicit explicit in a way that fosters a sense of hope, responsibility, and choice — the willingness to take charge of life as it is rather than waiting for the "right time" or the "lucky break" that will guarantee success. This is an essential feature of what it means to live "in the now", "in present time" — or simply to *live* as opposed to *preparing* to live.

The Counselor As Guide

A counselor, then, is a guide along the path of life, hopefully experienced enough and perceptive enough to be able to foster an ability to critically evaluate one's feelings and perceptions while at the same time inspiring a sense of trust in the unknown.

In the presence of such a third-eye perspective, couples are led to enhance their ability to live with uncertainty, ambiguity and paradox by becoming more conscious and choiceful about ways of mutually ordering and shaping a sometimes chaotic-appearing reality.

As a process for individual as well as couple development, couples counseling will ultimately also impact upon the surrounding human systems with which the couple interacts — friends, family, community. Each developmental issue confronted and resolved by a couple sets off a wave of reverberating changes in the individual and in the community such that as long as the communication flow continues between these different systemic levels (individual, couple, community) there will continue to be mutual accommodation and growth.

Development occurs, as discussed in earlier chapters, in stages. And as we pass from stage to stage we often encounter resistances to change. These resistance points — "stuck places" — are where the couples therapist focuses the work: encouraging clearer awareness where there had been confusion or avoidance; designing safe experiments or structured activities in order to help people contact unknown resources; modeling a view of reality which focuses on accepting *what is* and recognizing the *potential* inherent in the *present moment* rather than worrying about what "should be" or what "might happen."

The Impasse as Opportunity

The impasse felt by a couple is an *opportunity* for confronting new information in the relationship about an unmet need or an unused resource. The impasse exists because the forces pressing toward change (usually the awareness of a "problem" or an unmet need) are exactly equal to the forces resisting change (usually due to a perceived lack of inner or outer resources or to a "hanging on" to familiar patterns). And as long as this stasis is maintained, no change will occur. The "new input" needed from a counselor, then, is for something which will alter this stasis and break the impasse: a stronger, clearer realization of a need, perhaps; recognition that one possesses resources that were formerly unknown or unused; or perhaps simply a greater willingness to risk the unknown, to *stretch* oneself. Such new input into the couple's system fosters a reorganization of the forces in the situation at a more highly developed level of differentiation-integration since it is based on more complete information than was formerly available to the couple.

As the level of integration of increasingly differentiated parts increases, one's level of development increases. Thus, the term "development" is used synonymously with one's level of differentiation-integration, one's response-ability, or one's level of consciousness.

Each developmental stage has its own characteristic impulses and resistances as do the transition periods between stages. Couples usually enter counseling during a developmental "crisis" which they would like some assistance in resolving. They stop coming to therapy as soon as they have identified or developed their own internal resources for providing the sort of "new input" that the therapeutic structure has offered.

I'd like to detail a case illustration to show how the couples counseling process can work to heighten awareness, responsibility and choicefulness in a temporarily "stuck" situation. This case also illustrates how the process can help the couple use their relationship as a vehicle for both personal growth and community change, thus increasing their response-ability not only in their personal lives but in their social environment as well.

A couple in their mid-forties, with two teenage children, Janet and David had been living for several years in what might be called a "Power Struggle Stasis." Each was locked into familiar sex-role stereotypic behavior with regard to work and family responsibility; but the time was coming when all this would have to change.

They began counseling with a sense of impending crisis even in the midst of apparent stability. Janet had become increasingly anxious in recent months about the increasing amount of "free time" she had, now that the children have become less dependent on her. Wanting to find a job outside the home that would be satisfying and useful, she remained unsure of her abilities. She had used much of her free time in volunteer pursuits for community social agencies. David is the owner of a large local supermarket, who feels trapped in his job, and by the financial responsibilities of being the "head of the household." Janet and David were also feeling impatient with one another. She wished he would take more time from work to be with her and to relax, and he wanted her to stop complaining and find a new direction for herself that she would enjoy. She was critical of his overwork; he was pressuring her to find a job. They were also having difficulties in their sexual relationship. He experienced her as slow to respond and somewhat more passive than he would prefer. She experienced him as engaging in sex somewhat compulsively and mechanically. And so it went....

Awareness: What's Happening With Us?

They each experienced pain stemming from three interdependent sources: their own perceived "inadequacies", the annoying or unsupportive behavior of the other; and the impact of societal demands on their lives. Thus, the first stage of work — *experiencing the need* for change (on all three systemic levels: personal, interpersonal and societal) — was already taking place. This can be called the *Awareness* phase. During this stage in counseling, Janet and David "tell their stories" — how they feel about themselves, each other and their situation.

In the telling of their individual and couple stories, they related a history of: a brief "romantic" period, followed by an uneasy "power struggle" period of several years, and recently a semi-stable period of "accepting each other as we are" alternating with feelings of "we can't go on like this forever." Thus, although their relationship appeared to be relatively stable at least in the sense of its durability, the fact that they frequently reverted to the sort of blaming, "if-it-weren't-for-you" pattern characteristic of the power struggle stage, tells us that they needed to work more on "re-owning" their projected power struggles rather than focusing their efforts on changing their partner. Thus, the awareness (or first) phase of our work aimed at: (1) clarifying their individual and shared concerns; (2) helping them experience what needs were not being met in the relationship — for themselves and for each other; and (3) helping them experience how they mutually contributed to the "stuck" situation.

Thus, in Janet and David's case, even though they came to counseling with some awareness of what needs weren't being met, their experience had to be expanded to include an awareness of how "the other half" experienced the situation in order to help them to re-own their projected power struggle and achieve a more reliable stability in their relationship. One technique for helping to accomplish this awareness is the *role reversal*, in which I ask Janet to tell David's story as if she were David; while David "becomes" Janet and tells "her" story.

As we began this activity, it soon became obvious that it was extremely difficult for David to get in touch with feelings of passivity and lack of initiative in his attempt to tell Janet's story from Janet's viewpoint. As he played Janet, he would get very tense and slip out of role whenever he approached such expressions

of "weakness". In order to facilitate his playing "the passive one",
I decided to try another experiment, the "limb-lifting" exercise.
Here, I instructed him to lie quietly on the carpet, while I guided
her in slowly raising and lowering his head, arms, and legs, —
one-by-one — with an attitude of confident nurturance. This total
body awareness exercise helped David to more fully experience and
understand his resistances to passivity and receptiveness and to
come into closer contact with passive, out-of-control feelings in
himself. In subsequent role reversals, he found it much easier to
"be" Janet.

The role reversal technique is more than empathy training used
for facilitating interpersonal communication. It is, more significantly, a vehicle for contacting what Gestalt Therapist Jim Simkin
calls, "the other side of your coin", i.e., the aspect of a polarity
which is unconscious and therefore conspicuous by its absence. In
David's example, on the active-passive polarity, he tended to
consistently play the active role, having structured most of his life
(with society's blessings) around avoiding passivity or feelings of
being out-of-control. Thus, playing the passive role was a kind of
Gestalt "experiment", giving him the chance to contact an aspect
of his human potential of which he has been unaware. If, as Carl
Jung says, it is a psychological law that "what's unconscious gets
projected", then as long as David cannot experience passive,
receptive feelings, he will project these onto Janet. He will allow
her to carry all responsibility for these sorts of feelings in the
relationship, while he displays only his active side. This projection
mechanism generally leads to rigidified sex-role stereotypes such
as, "she's the accommodating one, and I'm the assertive one." It
also predictably leads to the "need" to project onto one's partner
those feelings which don't fit one's self-image (e.g., "weakness"
in David's case), and then to condemn her for "possessing" such
feelings. This, as we have seen, is the essential ingredient of the
power struggle.

Their successful working through of the role reversal process led
them beyond the Power Struggle and into a more dependable yet
flexible Stability Stage via several developments: both David and
Janet came into contact with a part of themselves that had formerly
been denied expression; each gained a clearer understanding of
and compassion for the other; and they both were confronted with
the complexity of developing an *integrated* response to their
situation — one which takes into account both passivity and activity

in a balanced way rather than rigidly and compulsively. An integrated response, as an individual or pair, is characterized neither by domination (too much) or deprivation (too little), but rather by a balance of activity-passivity or control-surrender in proportion to the changing needs of both people.

Generally, in working to develop such an integrated response, we encounter many "sub-personalities" or "parts" of each person's internal homeostatic system. The personality is actually a collection of such "characters". And just as the theatrical masks of comedy and tragedy symbolize, each "character in my drama" tends to be somewhat "two-faced." Personality can express itself either comically or tragically, playfully or seriously, actively or passively, forcefully or timidly, parentally or childishly.

The aim of working on awareness is to strengthen the individual and dyadic "observer". This ensures that even when one of my sub-personalities is expressing itself in terms of one of its two "faces", the *other side* is not forgotten or dis-owned, since I have an "observer" which functions to keep both sides aware of each other. Thus, responses tend more and more toward an *integration* of *both sides* of a formerly polarized aspect of our selves.

The Awareness phase of the work can involve at least one more task — that of discovering how the social context reinforces and helps to rigidify the problem. This awareness adds further dimension to the couples' perspective, contributing even more to their newly-achieved stability. A Gestalt technique for exploring this question is the "top-dog/under-dog" psychodramatic dialogue, in which the top-dog's script includes the forceful articulation of parental and societal expectations for appropriate "masculine" vs. "feminine" behavior (to use a popular example). The under-dog's script sounds a little like the naive or rebellious "child" who questions why things have to be done the way they have always been done. The under-dog speaks from a position of questioning the givens, with little apparent power in the situation, except for the power to resist. "Societies," "institutions", "authorities," — i.e., top-dogs — are often slow to respond to the needs of "deviant" or nonconforming individuals. The tension between the two, if it is *dynamic* (with energy flowing in both directions), can lead toward the development of a system with increasing tolerance for individual differences and responsiveness to individual needs, while at the same time fostering social consciousness. When power becomes concentrated at one end of the pole, however, the tension becomes *static*, resulting in domination or oppression.

In playing out the top-dog/under-dog dialogue, Janet and David took turns playing each other's top-dog, emptying the gunnysack of societal demands and expectations upon the person playing under-dog. The under-dog member of the pair resisted with every ploy in their repertoire — passive-aggressiveness, feigned compliance, excuse-making, temper tantrums, blaming, denial and so on — anything to avoid direct confrontation with the differences in perspective between them. The impasse thus created revealed to them the need for further expansion of the dialogue to include the *direct* expression of the anger they were feeling and a clear statement of *demands* on each other: "I want…" rather than "you should…" This awareness grew out of the frustration created in both of them upon seeing the impasse they were in. One of them could not get out of the impasse without the help of the other. Out of their frustration they began to ask for help. They began to recognize and take responsibility for their interdependence, as well as their differences.

This "interdependent different-ness," or "differentiated related-ness," as I like to call it, is an important fact of social life in these times. Women and men are coming to recognize, as they become more deeply aware of the polarizing effects of our social scripting, that "we're all in this together," that we need each other's help in transcending socially-programmed illusions about who we are and can be, and that since we are equally responsible as women and men for where we are today, we must take an equal share of the work necessary to transcend where we are.

Responsibility: Who's in Charge Here?

This awareness brings the couple to the *Responsibility* phase of the work — the recognition that no matter what personal and societal constraints one must live with, one is still responsible for the choices one makes regarding *how* to feel and behave: one can rebel against or conform to an oppressive social situation; one can express a difference of opinion to one's partner or decide not to express it; when such a difference has been confronted, one can fight, negotiate, or give in to the other. The work of this phase also involves the recognition of our equal responsibility for creating the present situation and our equal responsibility for re-creating and renewing our relationship.

In Janet and David's work, as they played each other's top-dog, they were able to see how easy it was to get coopted into "becoming" the other's projection of an oppressive social situation. If the community expected Janet to cook for the church bazaar, she imagined that David also expected this of her. And David actually experienced pressure from her, as well as from the community, to react this way.

In playing out the role of Janet's top-dog, while Janet faced him and resisted such pressure, David was able to recognize how much of this role really fit him and how much he needed to discard. The parts that he could consistently feel clear and energetic about expressing were the parts for which he came to own responsibility. The expressions that continued to feel forced or incongruent, he decided did not belong to him. These he recognized as Janet's or the community's expectations of how he *should* feel rather than his own feelings, and he refused to carry these projections any longer. This, of course, forced Janet and the community to confront and eventually re-own these attitudes as their own.

Janet then had to see how she had dealt with the conformist expectations of society: instead of "tasting" and "chewing" these expectations, she had "swallowed" them whole. She had "given in without resistance", without checking with herself to see if her own needs were pressing her toward the role of volunteer cook, for example, or if this was simply something she "was supposed to do". In confronting, through dialogue, "the community's and David's expectations" of her, she saw how she was indeed *oppressing herself*. She stopped secretly blaming him and started seeing him as a potential source of support for her "resistant" or under-dog side. She asked him to support her wish to say "no" to such community demands, thereby taking responsibility for both her wish to refuse and her need for help in doing so. Her need for a scapegoat disappeared as she took charge of her own life in this way.

Recognizing one's *freedom* to say "no" need not automatically result in *doing* so. Janet could've owned responsibility for not wanting to cook for the bazaar while still deciding she was willing to do so. Thus, *owning* our inner feelings need not make us *victims* to them — especially if we can develop our "observer function" so as not to become over-identified with any particular feeling. As it came about in this case, however, David discovered, through

witnessing Janet's assertion of her own independent wants, that *he*
actually wanted to try his hand at cooking for the bazaar in
question. He then had to confront his own projected expectation
that this was not usually done by a man; it was "women's work."
He had to decide that it was worth the possible cost to his public
image for him to express himself in this way. And he had to own
responsibility also for the fact that it mattered to him how other
people reacted to his "deviance" from the established norm.

Both Janet and David realized that taking responsibility for one's
own wants and feelings does not mean ignoring the wants and
feelings of others; nor does it make one invulnerable to these; nor
does it require that we act all alone without support from persons
who can help us. Taking responsibility requires the complex ability
to respond to our needs as well as our resources, to ourselves as
well as those with whom we choose to be interdependent. It grows
from an awareness that we have choice, which in turn evolves from
a well-developed "observer function" or sense of the whole — that
ability to see all of myself rather than to limit my perception (and
thus my sense of options) to one part.

Mutual Action: What Are We Going to Do About It?

Gaining *awareness* of *how* we limit ourselves and others, and
understanding our *responsibility* for *choosing* our behavior in a
potentially oppressive situation, can lead to hope or hopelessness:
to meeting life's challenge or to losing our courage. This brings us
to the threshold of the *Action* phase of the work. This phase in the
therapeutic process faces the couple with their commitment to their
relationship. True mutual action can only occur between partners
who have developed the ability to live with commitment and the
paradoxes that this implies. Action or commitment follows from
awareness and responsibility. When both members of the pair have
recognized the *choices* available to them, it is time to *decide:* to
commit one's energies in one direction and to give up certain other
options, based on some mutually-defined aim or sense of values.

In much of Janet and David's work, the commitment issue
centered on whether or not to commit their energies to the
relationship — to developing a mutually interdependent "we
system". During the Awareness and Responsibility phases of the
work, they had seen how much of their energy was used in
maintaining a state of ambivalence. Exploring the range of

possibilities within their multi-faceted polarities gave them a sense of what was and was not possible for them. They acquired a sense of their own preferences and limitations as well as of their social context, thus bringing them to the moment of truth.

At this point in the work, there may be a last desperate attempt to hide from what we already know — to go back to a naive stage of consciousness where we feel at the mercy of forces around us.

With Janet and David, ambivalence around staying in the relationship served as a focal point for resistance to commitment. The issue became trust. Janet expressed fear that David really didn't want to be with her — as evidenced by his preoccupation with his work and hobbies (an example of an unarticulated tension between "staying vs. straying" — one of the central paradoxes of a committed relationship). She mistrusted his affirmations of affection and commitment. She imagined that he felt "trapped". In this scripted scenario, Janet had been playing the role of "doubter", while David played the role of "reassurer," (another "game" in their dyad)

In exploring this polarity using the Gestalt dialogue process, I asked Janet to play the part of David: first, as she *feared* he felt; then, as she *wished* he felt; and finally as, *"any other person" might* feel in response to such accusations about lack of commitment. This gave her the experience that she could *create her own reality* according to any image she chose. She saw that when she "imaged" David ("saw" him with her mind's eye) as rejecting, he "became" rejecting. When she "imaged" him as loving, he "became" loving. And when she "imaged" him as impatient with her mistrust, but still supportive, he "became" this as well. Checking with David himself, she learned that this is indeed what happened in their life together. Janet could, to some extent, "create" him as rejecting, loving, impatient, or whatever, and he could do the same with her. Positive expectations engender positive outcomes. Negative expectations engender negative outcomes. Thus, her sense of responsibility was expanded to include: first, her ability to alter her responses at will; and second, her ability to consciously choose the effect she wished to have, according to a mutually-beneficial aim.

Once this realization has been assimilated (and it may require many confrontations with similar sequences for it to be understood), Janet and David can no longer avoid *acting upon the world* with conscious intention. They cannot act as if they are victims — in the relationship or in the larger society. They understand that to behave as if one is powerless *makes* one powerless. It is simply a way of avoiding responsibility for creating one's own life; in other words, avoiding commitment.

When two people are able to achieve self-responsibility (via re-owning projected powers), and mutual commitment (via learning to live with paradox and ambiguity), they can become a strong support system for one another in confronting and changing an unsupportive or spiritually impoverished community or social context. They can begin to re-define themselves according *to what they want and value* rather than according to what they imagine others expect from them. They can "image" and thereby create the higher aspects of their humanity rather than imagining that they are trapped by social convention into repeating their self-constricting patterns. And whenever individuals or a pair of individuals are able to transcend existing cultural categories, this is when they are also able to have a historically significant impact on their culture. This, then, is the path to social transformation — individuals acting collectively and co-creatively in ways that transcend the commonly held self-limiting beliefs and self-fulfilling prophecies about human beings. Only when we truly *learn from experience* and are willing to *change* accordingly, do we move onto a more refined stage of development. If we refuse to let go of old patterns and beliefs, we are destined to repeat the same scripts over and over and over. Society's and humanity's evolution depends on dyads and groups who are willing to stop repeating the past.

Thus, Janet and David, after months of struggle against their internalized societal constraints and role expectations, decided to create a lifestyle that fit them. They decided to commit themselves to the relationship and to making it work for them rather than being scared off by the sacrifices that this would require of them. For Janet and David the lifestyle change did not mean dropping out and moving to Alaska as homesteaders. Their changes were at the same time less grandiose and more courageous, since they occurred within the community where the couple had always lived. The major change involved the way they structured their time. David arranged to pay an assistant to manage the store half-time, so he could have this time available for other things he enjoyed doing: playing with his family, reading, sports, being with friends, sharing more loving and tender time with Janet. Janet also began to relax some of her externally-imposed demands on herself; she decided not to pursue a career as such, realizing that this had been an expectation of David's but not something she really wanted; she did accept more responsibility for helping him with the store; and she began to develop her skill as a photographer, an avenue of creativity to which she had been postponing commitment for several years.

Social Implications of Personal Change

As these lifestyle changes evolved over time, Janet, who had been the more "social" of the pair, became more involved in her photography; and David, who had been more achievement-oriented, became more interested in sharing quality time with good friends. This represented a kind of role reversal for the couple — a breaking free of the stereotyped roles around which they had structured their time for most of their lives.

David and Janet saw their lifestyle change as not simply a personal matter. It was also an act of social and political significance — a statement about the individual's power in a society where most individuals act as if they are victims to a repressive structure. They represented, for their community to witness and participate in, the power of individuals to "image" the kind of world they wanted, and to find their own path in co-creating such a world. By remaining in the community and in dialogue with it, they maximized their impact in this regard. Others in their social milieu were confronted daily with the changes they had made, participated in their struggles, and were thus also changed in the process.

This little vignette of a couple's journey to actualize their own inner vision with the support of a couples therapist seems quite a modest effort in the direction of personal liberation and societal change — when we think of all the changes that need to be made. Yet it is becoming more and more clear that a healthy society can only be created by whole and healthy individuals — persons who "own" their power and interdependence rather than projecting blame for their situation onto the spouse or the "system". Thus, the consciousness development process fostered by working through the various crises of an intimate couple relationship provides individuals with the sense of commitment and response-ability necessary to transform personal and collective life. The self-differentiation and self-responsibility process fostered in moving from stability to commitment and co-creation on the couples journey is mirrored on the societal level in the couple's struggle to differentiate itself from conformist and stereotypic definitions of what it means to be a couple.

As a pair of individuals gain the courage to be, the couple system is strengthened also in its ability to differentiate itself from the cultural status quo. And if both self- and couple-differentiation processes are occurring in dialogue with the surrounding community, the resulting mutual accommodations will undoubtedly produce social as well as personal change.

The social activist period of the 60's taught us that major societal restructuring cannot occur when the individuals involved feel impotent in their own lives — when they are "imaging" themselves as victims rather than as actors.

We are seeing more and more clearly the profound inter-dependence between all persons, groups, and nations — as well as between all forms of life on the planet. We are coming to view the man-woman relationship as one link in a larger chain of interdependent systems. It is in a sense our link to a more self-transcendent experience of identity.

Thus, we must empower "the other" if we ourselves are to have power. We must give love if we are to receive love. We must be always open to change and new creation, if we are to find stability.

The process of couples counseling is therefore not only a way to help individuals in relationship. It is also a way of fostering a greater understanding of the principles that guide all human relationships. As we work to re-own projections and to balance the male and female polarities within, we come to value and respect our differences. As we learn how to integrate self and other interest in our relationship, we come to more deeply understand human interdependence. And as we come to understnad the principle of interdependence as it operates in our dyad, we move toward a realization of our rightful place in relationship to the ecology of the planet as well. ·

Confronting the social system from the supportive framework of a strong couple relationship provides an alternative to the models which have already been tried. Such a relationship is one in which individuals have experienced risking *confrontation* with a significant other person, (whose wants at a given moment may be *different* from one's own) and who have *negotiated* a lifestyle which empowers both.

Belonging to a "we system" helps to overcome the potential feelings of isolation common when relating to large and impersonal social institutions. In a sense the relationship is a *refuge*. Yet it is also a *link* to the larger social system, reminding us always of our interdependence with others. It is unlikely that I will retreat into my own view of the world when I am in a relationship where the reality of the "we system" is always a product of *your* world perspective in combination with *mine*.

Working out an intimate relationship is not just a path of differentiation from the social maya (or illusion). It is also in a sense a *preparation* for relating to the world. It affords the opportunity to experience the inevitable power struggles of human relationships — the politics of sex and aggression — up close, first hand. It confronts us dramatically and inescapably with our interdependence as human beings: if half the world (or half of the couple) is getting rich off the deprivation of the other half, no one can be satisfied.

In the intimacy of couple and family life, these awarenesses cannot be avoided. If I hurt or oppress you from a position of greater socially-sanctioned power, I'll feel the repercussions of this act somehow, even if only because I have to take care of you when you get sick. The Easterners call it the Law of Karma. Christians quote the Bible, "you reap what you sow." There is a saying in the Afro-American community, "what goes 'round, comes 'round." "And in the end", say the Beatles, "the love you take is equal to the love you make."

The couple relationship may be the interpersonal unit most suited for transforming self and society to a new consciousness: a consciousness where interpersonal differences are seen as a source of learning and growth; where conflicts between the individual and society can be negotiated from a dependable support base, and where the individual can experience human interdependence in a way that leads to seeing problems as the shared responsibility of all parts of the system.

chapter ten

THE COUPLES
GROUP INTENSIVE

A promising alternative to psychotherapy for the couple relationship is the group intensive. Couples who wish to explore other ways of enhancing their relationship may find some advantages in this approach. In contrast to the traditional psychotherapy format of one to two hours per week, spaced over several weeks to a year or more, the group intensive format occurs in the span of one or two weekends. The process is still guided by a trained couples therapist, but since the work is done in a group rather than in the privacy of the consulting room, less attention is given by the therapist to each particular couple. There is more chance to learn from the experience of other couples, however, so the group intensive format has some advantages over the psychotherapy model.

Both models see the couple relationship as a path toward individual and couple development, and both models see the couple relationship as a mutual support system for impacting upon the larger social system and the world.

The group intensive format brings into the here and now a

temporary "larger social system," thereby immediately confronting the couple with both the supportive and the potentially
confining aspects of belonging to a community. This feature also
brings with it the opportunity to view couple relationships in
general from a social systems perspective, offering each person the
direct experience of the sociological forces which impinge on
couples and individuals in our society. Participants get perspective
on some of the more "universal" aspects of being part of a couple
— or of being a wife, a husband, a lover, a partner, a breadwinner,
or a parent. They have a chance to see how they are alike, and how
they are different from other couples, and from others in their
respective relationship-roles. Such perspective is often useful in
promoting a clearer understanding of the systemic sociological
forces at work in determining how people behave. This
understanding helps to balance the psychological, psychohistorical
understanding which is gained through the process of "re-owning
projections" mentioned in connection with more traditional couples
therapy.

Thus, the group intensive workshop provides a context for
enhancing sociological, as well as psychological and spiritual
understanding. It shows participants how they have been
acculturated with numerous self-limiting and stereotypic beliefs
about their potential as humans, simply due to such social factors
as "the climate of the times", their ethnic or racial heritage, their
gender, their income and so on.

As is the case with more psychologically-oriented work,
enhancing one's understanding of social systems (as they impact on
individuals and couples) is a consciousness-raising process. It
involves the development of awareness, responsibility, choice, and
the capacity for shared commitment to action. These steps in the
working-through process may occur at whatever developmental
stage the couple is — whether they are dealing with issues
involving romance, power, stability, commitment, or co-creation.

Typically, the group intensive workshops that I conduct begin
with a self-assessment (or diagnosis) process to help couples
ascertain their present stage of development. Next comes a series
of structured group activities designed to enhance functioning at
each couple's current developmental stage, and to introduce some
experiences associated with the next probable stage on the path.
Most couples need some workshop time to alternate these two sets
of activities (present stage work and next probable stage work) in

order to gain confidence in their ability to move from familiar to less familiar territory. Toward the latter part of the workshop, participants are guided in the formulation and practice of action plans, affirmations, or self-observation strategies utilizing new insights and skills.

In order to demonstrate what actually happens in a couples group intensive, I'd like to describe a recent workshop which I conducted. The workshop took place over two consecutive weekends — Saturdays and Sundays, 9 AM through 6 PM, in a large, carpeted room at a local community college. Forty couples attended.

Couples had come expecting to enhance their personal, interpersonal and spiritual development through the growth of the couple relationship.

First Weekend

As couples milled into our meeting room that first morning, there was an entire "graffitti wall" covered with white butcher paper which had been divided into two parts — one column headed by the words "We are..." and another by the words "I am..." As couples began to fill the room, they were invited also to fill the wall with their immediate responses to these two-sentence stems. "I am excited... We are depressed" read one entry. Others were: "I am alone... We are all one;" "I am confused... We are doubly confused!"; "I am I, You are you,... We are you and I"; "I am together... We are split."

When the wall had been almost completely covered with such graffitti, we as a newly forming temporary community of seekers had a fairly good notion of how others in the room were feeling. We saw that we were not alone in our feelings and that there were a variety of viewpoints in the room. We were also beginning to develop one of the major themes of any couple relationship: the "me vs. we" or "independence vs. interdependence" issue, and we were engaging in the initial phase of the self-assessment process, which would guide our work during the early part of the workshop.

Building on the graffitti wall data, we began our individual and couple self-assessment. First individually and then with our partners, we answered the following self-inventory questions:

   a. When do I feel most fulfilled in this relationship?
   b. When do I feel least fulfilled in this relationship?
   c. What do I do and what does my partner do which contri-

butes to such fulfillment and lack of fulfillment?

d. What would need to change in my own and in my partner's behavior to transform the least fulfilling situations into more fulfilling ones?

e. What am I learning in this situation even if nothing changes?

After each pair had shared their answers to these items, I called for a no-talking break during which we created another "I am...We are" graffiti wall on the wall adjacent to the first one. This break period allowed individuals to center within themselves, in contrast to the momentum that had been created toward focusing on their partnership. It also gave them time to reflect upon and digest what was for some a fairly intense dose of interpersonal contact. And it gave the entire community a public view of our private processes, adding to the growing feeling of safety and support for self-disclosure.

My rationale for alternating periods of sharing (or contact) with periods of alone time (or withdrawal) comes from my conviction that a couple relationship seeks to nurture both the self and the partner, neither to the exclusion of the other; and from my experience that most people tend to get overly focused on either self-interest or partner's interest and have a difficult time balancing the tension between these. Thus, my design validates from the outset that both self-interest and partner-interest are important and in fact necessary in relationships. (Eventually we learn that the tension between the two can be creative and synergetic rather than conflictful, but this insight usually comes later on in the work.)

After everyone has had a chance to mill around and read the new entries on the graffiti wall, participants are asked to gather into groups of four — two couples to a group. In this structure couples begin to develop their ability to give and receive third-party consultation. For openers, each person is asked to "discuss with your partner your reactions to what you've just read on the graffiti wall," and to "share how you feel about your own contribution to the wall when seen in the context of others." While couple #1 are sharing, couple #2 listens and observes without comment. Then couple #2 shares while couple #1 observes. After both couples have shared and observed, they are asked to give each other feedback according to a very simple set of guidelines: "Describe to the couple you were observing in as much concrete detail as you can, what you saw and heard during their sharing. Be as much like a 'video-taped replay' as you can, presenting *observable data* rather than your own *feelings or interpretations.*'' Following these simple instructions allows couples to build trust and acceptance (since no judgements or interpretations are given) and to gain a feeling of being truly helpful to other people's growth (since very rarely do we get an opportunity to see ourselves as others see us). The ''no interpretations'' guideline is an important teaching device for helping people learn to develop their actions from concrete experience rather than from ideas or fantasies of ''how one ought to act.''

A major feature of the couples group intensive is the two-couple quartet structure in which couples discuss issues and feelings with their partners and receive feedback from the other couple after each group activity. During the early stages of the workshop, couples join with a different couple each time the quartet structure is used. Later on, more stable on-going quartets are formed, providing a consistent and developing support system for each couple. Participants are encouraged to continue meeting with their quartets beyond the termination of the two-weekend intensive. (Those who have done so report that such follow-up support has been a major factor in keeping their relationships alive and growing.)

Following the large group *warm-up* via the graffitti wall and the introduction to the process of sharing in pairs and quartets, the ''self and relationship inventory'' begins. This is the first activity in the *diagnosis* phase of the work. Next comes *problem-solving*, and then *action planning*, with an emphasis in the final phase on transfer of learning to the backhome environment and the building of a dependable support network for sustaining learning and growth. This, then, is an overview of the workshop: warm-up, diagnosis, problem-solving (emphasizing practicing new skills in the here and now), and action planning.

The rest of this chapter is an outline of activities we engaged in during the two-weekend intensive, and commentary on how some of the material was used by participants.

I. Diagnosis: The diagnostic/self-assessment phase of the workshop includes the following activities:

A. *Introductory Mini-lecture*

Participants are reminded that our present wants and values are determined partly by past experiences and partly by our hopes and dreams for the future. The purpose of the diagnostic phase is noted as providing a structure for assessing individual and couple strengths, limitations, values and goals so that the later work on problem-solving and action-planning can be based upon realistically perceived needs and resources.

B. *Self-inventory*

1. *A Life Line* exercise asks: "On a large piece of paper, draw a line representing your individual life. Put a check mark on it to symbolize where you are now. Embellish your line in any way you wish, showing high and low points or other significant events in your life.

Now, discuss together for a few minutes why you drew your line as long as you did, why you put the check mark where you did, and any other features of your drawing. Some people will focus more on chronological age, while others will place more emphasis on emotional or psychological forces or events."

After we have discussed this activity sufficiently, we go on to the next activity.

2.*Who Am I* guides participants to: "On ten separate slips of paper, write ten different answers to the question: Who am I? You may think of yourself in terms of your social or professional roles, in terms of qualities you have — both positive and negative — or in terms of a combination of these. When you have finished, look over what you have written and think about what you would be and how you would feel if you eliminated any one of your items.

Now, rank order your slips of paper, placing at the top of the pile those items you consider to be most essential to you. At the bottom, place those self-descriptions that you could most do without and still not lose your essential quality.

After you have both finished your rank ordering, share and discuss them with one another."

3. *Autobiography* goes like this: "Look again at your 'lifeline' drawing. Focus your attention on the part of the drawing that is ahead of you, the future. Let your imagination go to a point in the future most distant from where you are now. What might a brief

biography of you include at that time? What would you like it to include? Write a brief autobiography as it might appear at that future point in time in a *Who's Who* listing. Write it as you would like it to be, containing things you want to accomplish in your life, as if you have actually already done them. Be realistic, but not overly modest.''

''Now share your autobiographies with your partner and discuss them. Go back to your ''Who am I?'' list and add any additional statements that might be true of you or become true of you in the future.''

(*We usually take a break before going on to the next activity.*)

4. *Life Inventory:* ''The life inventory consists of several elements and generally requires at least an hour's time. Its purpose is to look at all the things you do and would like to do, your *resources* or what you *have*, and your *needs*, or what you *would like to have*. The inventory will help you display all of yourself, in terms of your activities and values, what you do and what you say you'd like to do. It will give you a sort of map of your life in terms of a number of elements which may or may not be overlapping.

''The first element is called *Peak Experiences*, the events in your life that have really mattered to you in terms of making you feel glad to be alive. These will be your high moments, the times of your life that are remembered as having been really great, the times that have made you feel most worthwhile or alive or whole.

''As these peak events occur to you, just describe them spontaneously to your partner. Your partner will serve as interviewer and recorder for you while you are free to just think and respond. After you have inventoried your peak experiences for about ten minutes, it will be your partner's turn to do so, while you serve as recorder. Follow this same interviewee-recorder procedure for the remaining life inventory elements as well.

''The next part of the life inventory is called, *Things I Do Well.* Think of things you do which are very meaningful to you. Some overlap may occur here with your first list, peak experiences. On the other hand, some of the things you do well may actually be of little interest to you. This is often a hard list to compile because it competes with our cultural expectation to be modest. Try to overcome this inhibition.

"The next element is, *Things I Do Poorly*. This list should contain things you want to do, need to do, or have done, not things in which you have no interest. It should be a list of things you do poorly or without zest that for some reason or other you need to do.

"Then we come to, *Things I Would Like to Stop Doing*. This listing could include things you are required to do and would like to stop doing, as well as things you feel more responsible for choosing to do. Just focus on any ways that you spend your time and energy which seem unsatisfying or unproductive.

"This is followed by, *Things I Would Like To Learn To Do Well*. This might be a list of desired skills, whether personal, relationship-oriented, or job-related. It might also related to an avocation or leisure-time activity.

"The next element is, *Peak Experiences I Would Like To Have*. These are some things you imagine you would like to have happen to you which have not.

"*Values to be Realized* is an element less clear than the others. Values mean different things to different people. It could include having money, serving others, being in a loving friendship, working with children, living more spontaneously, and so on. 'Values,' while not very tangible, generally refer to things which we feel will enhance our sense of meaning or worth.

"The last element is, *Things I'd Like to Start Doing Now*. The objective here is to explore some of the things you may have been putting 'off, but which you really want to start doing. It could include anything from growing a beard to asking more for what I want, to starting my own business."

C. *Couple Sharing*

"After you have both completed your life inventories, look over what you have each said for similarities and differences between your values and goals. Share your feelings about these.

D. *Sharing in the Total Group*

In summing up the self-inventory work, individuals are invited to share in the total group to help promote a sense of community and shared support. It is important for the therapist to listen especially at this time for expressions of distress over "how different I am" (from one's partner or from what seems to be the group norm). In eliciting responses, the therapist encourages the sharing of a wide range of feelings (both pleasant and unpleasant) with an attitude of acceptance, in order to help people realize that whatever differences exist among people are okay and are just more "grist for the mill".

E. Couple Inventory

Here, each couple engages conjointly in the Life Line, Who Am I? (in this case, "Who are We?"), Autobiography, and Life Inventory activities (as in 1-4 above). Since each activity is done as a "we system," instead of drawing one's *personal* life line, the partners together draw a line which represents their *shared* journey.

F. Sharing in Quartets

Once again, consulting partners are instructed to simply listen and "play back the tape" of what they saw and heard, without interpretation or evaluation and *above all without attempting to be "helpful."*

G. Sharing in the Total Group

Here participants are asked to create together a "verbal graffitti wall" by singing out one-by-one their completion of the sentence stem, "I learned..."

This focuses the group's energy on the positive value of increasing communication in spite of the fact that as we open up more to each other, we generally become more aware of differences (and potential conflicts) which will need resolution or acceptance before we can take action toward a shared goal.

H. Taking a Case History of Our Relationship

The purpose of this activity is to assess the developmental issues the couple has already confronted and weathered and to look more closely at which issues are currently pressing for attention and resolution.

This interviewing is done in consulting quartets, with Couple #1 interviewing Couple #2 (after which #2 interviews #1) using the following questions:

1. How, of all the millions of people in the world, did you two find each other?

2. Do you remember what first attracted you to your partner?

3. How long ago was that?

4. Which of these sources of initial attraction still operate in your relationship? (Which have you found to be based more on a romantic ideal than on things as they really are? Which have simply changed or are no longer important?)

5. How else has the relationship developed or changed since that time? Can you recall any significant "crises" or "rites of passage" you've shared (such as those sometimes brought on by birth, death, re-location, job change, or "coming of age")?

6. Most couples find that they consistently differ on certain attitudes, values, or ways of doing things. Can you think of some ways in which you two rather consistently see or do things differently?

7. How do you deal with these differences?

8. How did you develop this way of handling your differences? What sorts of things did you try before arriving at this method?

9. What other sources of conflict can you think of that confront or have in the past confronted the two of you? How have you learned to handle these conflicts?

10. Are there some things that continue to bother you about him or her? Are you trying to change this or have you decided to live with it?

11. Would you be willing to think back for a moment to the various fights or conflicts you have had? Could you describe in detail one of your more memorable ones? (How did it start? Who took which position? How did it get resolved? Is this typical of your way of resolving differences generally?)

12. Do you ever fight or disagree about money? What is likely to be the substance of this disagreement?

13. How is your relationship structured in terms of finances? (Who brings money in? How does it get spent? Who decides how and where to spend it? Does this vary depending on the area in question?)

14. If you could restructure your financial arrangement in any way you desired, how would you want to change things?

15. Do you ever fight or have conflicts about sex? What is likely to be the substance of such a fight?

16. If you could restructure your sex life in any way you wished, how would you want to change things?

17. Are there things you used to fight about but no longer do? How has this change come about?

18. In every relationship/family certain roles or tasks have to get done, some by one person, some cooperatively. Can you describe who usually does each of the following? cooking; cleaning house; home repairs; laundry; driving on trips; putting kids to bed; attending to kids; negotiating with school; negotiating with banks or credit agencies; negotiating with household service agencies or people; paying bills; maintaining contact with mutual friends.

19. In a couple's personal life certain roles or tasks also tend to be carried out most often by one member or the other. In your relationship who usually does each of the following: starts a fight; makes up; soothes hurt or angry feelings; initiates sex; suggests recreational activities; initiates exchanges of warmth or affection; initiates discussion of ideas; initiates discussion of personal problems (about self, other, family, friends); asks for time to do something alone or which excludes the partner?

20. It is often said that every act or decision has both a cost and a benefit. What are the most important benefits that you get out of being a part of this relationship?

21. What do you give up in order to belong to the relationship? What are the costs?

22. Do you ever experience conflict between your commitment to work, hobbies, or other relationships and your commitment to this relationship? How do you deal with this?

23. Do you consider yourself to be in a committed relationship? What does this mean in terms of what you can expect from one another?

24. When did you realize or decide that you were thus committed? Was there an identifiable turning point or did it evolve more subtly?

25. Have any events or crises occurred since that time to threaten the security of this commitment?

26. Have any events occurred which strengthened it?

27. Do the two of you have any joint commitments to projects, work, hobbies, or social causes *outside* the relationship or family? What are these?

28. Do they seem to add to or subtract from the bond between you? How?

After each couple has been interviewed by their "consultants," I ask for data feedback from the group question by question. This gives us an overview of what issues couples have confronted and are currently dealing with and it serves as a cross check on the validity of the theory to be presented next.

I. *"Developmental Stages of Coupling" mini-lecture*

This lecture presents descriptive data from previous research and the group's own mini-study, showing how the couples journey develops and changes over time: focusing on issues of romance and power in the earlier stage, and stability, commitment and co-creation later on. The material for this presentation is drawn from the first eight chapters of this book, modified and up-dated by any new or discrepant findings in the present sample of interviews.

J. *What issue(s) are most important for us as a couple right now?*

In response to this question, couples are asked to reflect on their responses during the interview and to arrive at an assessment of their current developmental stage or stages (in cases where several issues seem equally salient). There is also the option of arriving at a *new* label for the issue of primary concern other than one of the five offered (issues of *romance, power, stability, commitment,* or *co-creation.*)

K. *Sharing in Quartets*

After arriving at a "self-diagnosis," couples are asked to share this with their consultant partners. Consultants ask clarifying questions to help ascertain how the self-diagnosis was arrived at (i.e., the specifics on which their inferences regarding developmental stage were based).

L. *Large Group Sharing*

As a wrap-up to the Diagnostic Phase of the workshop, couples again contribute to a large graffitti wall which has been divided into five sections: romance, power, stability, commitment, co-creation. Couples are asked to look through their notes taken while interviewing their quartet partners to find "quotable quotes" to illustrate the concerns typical of a particular stage. For example, under the *Romance* heading might be written the quotation, "We were going to give each other everything our parents never gave us." Or under *Commitment*, "If I put out energy in her direction, it always comes back to me. I get what I give."

The diagnosis phase of the workshop generally consumes Friday evening through Saturday evening in the workshop schedule. Couples return on Sunday morning to begin the problem-solving phase.

II. Problem-Solving: The problem solving phase of the workshop includes the following activities:

A. *A Mini-Lecture* on what to expect from this phase of the work and how it will build on yesterday's diagnosis.

B. *Structured Activities*, which take place during the Sunday morning session, consist of a series of five exercises, sequentially presented, highlighting the issues of the five major developmental stages. (See Chapter 8 for a selection of the type of activities offered in this session.)

C. *Re-assessment of "Where We're At"*

After participants have sampled at least five structured activities highlighting developmental "crises" that couples may confront, they meet in consulting quartets to review learnings and identify issues needing further work. The instructions for this re-assessment period are: "With your partner, and with your consultants observing and ready to 'play back the tape,' review your experiences of the morning session, noting especially any events which caused you to feel either very energized or very stuck. Once you have agreed on the event or events, see if you can, with the help of your consultants, find a *theme* which could characterize what the issue, dilemma or *question* is for which you two are seeking resolution or clarification." (On the subject of "how to identify your theme or question;" I usually take questions from the audience and use particular cases to illustrate my message.)

"Note that question on a piece of newsprint and when both couples in the quartet have your question written down, post these sheets of paper on the wall where everyone can see them." (I also give participants the option of drawing a picture that illustrates their theme in addition to or instead of a verbal presentation.)

D. *Individual Couple Work*

By Sunday afternoon everyone has had a chance to discuss and digest the experiences of the morning, to make some sense out of them, to hear how their partners and others experienced them, and to see posted on the wall the questions, issues, and unfinished business generated by them. We (including I as facilitator) have a sense of which issues are most salient in this particular group as a basis for the afternoon's work.

When we meet as a large group in the afternoon, I open with a mini-lecture, "The Question as 90% of the Answer," supporting the courage and clarity it takes to ask meaningful, searching questions about our relationships. I also state my conviction, with supporting data, that when a person can identify a question that he or she really wants to answer, the answer is not far away. Responsible question-asking is a valuable resource in a relationship; for in the process of trying to find and agree on a question (which concerns both and to which *both* seek an answer), many other questions are answered (especially those for which one party had more information than the other).

I also stress that not all problems have solutions and not all questions have "answers" in the usual sense; life is paradoxical, and often learning to accept its inevitable dilemmas is the key to happiness and contentment. It may be more important to learn how to live with uncertainty and ambiguity than to learn how to eradicate it. Thus, as we get further into the weekend we begin to penetrate the deeper and subtler dimensions of relationship.

For the remainder of the afternoon, couples are invited to come to the front of the room with me to work on their question (or their picture). This is very much like "hot seat" work in Gestalt Therapy* where one couple works as the rest look on, identifying and silently doing their own work.

The total group does get involved from time to time in any of several ways: as participants in Gestalt "experiments" or psychodramatic role plays; as significant others for a person

---

*See Fritz Perls, *Gestalt Therapy Verbatim*. Moab, Utah: Real People Press, 1969.

"making rounds" or making some sort of public statement requiring an audience; and as participating group members when the couple's issue develops into a group issue*.

My work with each couple starts with a clear statement from them about how they would like me to participate with or guide them in the exploration of their question. They, of course, re-state the question as well as their notion of how they think things will be different once they've answered their question. Thus, we begin with a contract of clearly expressed expectations of themselves and of me. After this is accomplished, the work proceeds in any of a variety of ways.

A case example will illustrate: Phil and Carolyn (a couple in their late thirties) walked slowly to the front of the room and almost whispered to me their question, "How can we allow each other to have occasional sexual friends without creating too much stress in our relationship?"

They reported that they had been essentially monogamous for the five years they'd been together, and felt that they were working mostly on issues of stability. What they hoped for in achieving an answer to their question was to "arrive at a place where no outside intrusions can destroy the relationship we've invested so much in." They valued security, yet they also wanted the freedom to have other special friends outside the relationship.

This is such a popular issue with couples that you could hear a pin drop in the room as Phil and Carolyn and I formed our contract for working together:

Susan: "And what do you hope to get from me with regard to your question? What do you *really* want — even if you think it may be too much to ask for. Be as demanding as you can imagine being."

Carolyn: "I want you to *make* Phil *hear me* — that I'm not going

*For example, during one group intensive, a man and a woman working up front began hurling stereotypic attacks aimed at "how men are" and "how women are". It became clear that the entire group was emotionally involved in this encounter and it was also clear that total group participation would lend perspective to the conflict. I invited men and women in the group to stand at two opposite sides of the room and continue to hurl stereotypic remarks at each other, exaggerating these to fully test the limits of their emotions. The results of this intergroup encounter were an increased feeling of support within each group and empathy between groups. And most importantly, the catharsis paved the way for some hearty laughter shared by all.

Here, too, we have a concrete example of a "dilemma" (the differences in perspective of men and women) which needs to be *accepted* rather than "solved."

to leave him — I just want to go out with other men once in a while when I go out-of-town on business trips."

Phil: "And I want you to help Carolyn see that I have good reason to be afraid of losing her — she's a rare woman and a lot of men are going to want her if they really get to know her as I do."

Carolyn: (sharply) "Look, Phil, no one is ever going to know me the way you do..."

Susan: (interrupting) "It looks like you're ready to go at it, Carolyn, but first I want to let you know that I'm available as a consultant to help you hear each other and to help you see yourselves as your partner sees you. Is that what you want from me? Can you cooperate with me toward that end?"

Carolyn: "That sounds fine."

Phil: "Yes, that would satisfy me. And I'll try not to be too difficult to get through to."

Susan: "Okay, Let's start by just talking to each other about the issue. If you get stuck, you can ask for some consultation. If you don't, just go ahead and resolve things between yourselves."

As Phil and Carolyn began to dialogue about the question of outside relationships, it became clear that they kept missing each other's viewpoint. It looked to me as if he saw the issue as one of *control* — it was a situation that made him feel out of control; whereas she saw it as an issue of *freedom* — she felt it gave her more freedom to have the option of outside sexual relationships.

Roles had become polarized, so that it seemed she was the one asking for "freedom" and he was the one asking for "security". Neither was aware of "the other side of their coin" — that he too often wanted similar "freedom" and that she also often wanted to be closer and more "secure."

This sort of polarization is what generally leads to an impasse in a couple's communication. And it was here that they asked for some consultation from me. I entered by asking each what they were experiencing:

Phil: "I'm feeling afraid...afraid of Carolyn's anger, I think."

Carolyn: "And I'm not feeling especially angry...mostly I'm feeling like withdrawing...very passive."

Susan: "I'd like to work with each of you individually for a few minutes to help you get clearer with yourself before going back to your partner.

"Let's you and I work first, Phil. And what I'd like you to do is imagine Carolyn in this empty chair and continue the two-part dialogue, but this time, you play both parts.''

In the process of this ''inner dialogue'' role-play, Phil was able to experience the voice in himself (at first it was played as Carolyn's voice) that wanted freedom to have other relationships.

And when Carolyn had completed her inner dialogue, she was able to identify a new (to her awareness) voice in herself — a voice that wanted both more control in the relationship and more closeness. Thus, she was able to own those feelings that she had formerly attributed to Phil.

The struggle that had been occurring *between* the pair they discovered to be almost identical to the struggle occurring *within* each of them. Thus, each was able to experience their desire for *both* freedom and security instead of projecting one side of the argument onto the partner. This led to an immediate recognition of their *shared responsibility* for the problem, and to a *sense of perspective* on how they had gotten to where they were — how they had mutually *''chosen''* this particular problem as a way to learn more about the freedom-security issue both individually and as partners.

What they had learned so far was that a person can feel *both* needs at once — that it's not necessarily a case of *either-or*. They also saw that they each had a *range* of responses along the freedom-security continuum and that their balance point (or preference) on this continuum changes from time to time, such changes being related partly to one's inner state and partly to environmental pressures (especially those coming from one's partner).

New light was shed on the realities of *paradox, change,* and *shared responsibility* in Phil and Carolyn's work. They still had some more problem-solving to do together, but they had worked through a major impasse and felt energized and ready for the next steps in their journey.

At the close of their work, I invited other particpants to share their experience of the work. Many said they had resonated to both the content and process (the *what* and *how*) of Phil and Carolyn's issue. And many substituted other content issues (e.g., saving vs. spending money) and worked silently on their own or in their journals. (I suggest to all participants that they keep a journal during the intensive for writing feelings and learnings and for doing one's own work silently. The journal is an ideal place to carry on an inner dialogue, for example.)

E. *Quartet Work*

After several couples have worked with me in the large group context, we again divide into quartets to summarize learning and identify unfinished business. This is a kind of re-assessment of our goals and self-contracts, in which each person takes about 10 minutes of "air time" to achieve closure on the weekend for him or herself.

Couples are asked to meet with their quartets once during the following week to simply exchange information on any new perspectives they have gained on their question(s) since the weekend. The suggested structure for the first hour of this meeting is that partners will talk with each other about new learnings or questions while the consultant couple observes. If a communication impasse occurs, they are instructed to note in their journals how they are experiencing the impasse and then to put it aside until the following weekend, where they will have time for more problem-solving and for action planning.

F. *Large Group Closing Session*

Here, the focus is on reviewing the shared joy (when things are going along smoothly) and the shared learning (when conflict occurs) that we've experienced during the weekend. Using a guided self-reflection structure, I ask individuals to recall: (1) their original self-contract; (2) the question they mutually decided upon; (3) the high points and low points (in terms of energy or learning) of the weekend; and (4) what they have learned about themselves in the context of a relationship.

We close with the sharing of "I learned..." statements in the total group.

Second Weekend

A. *Problem Solving*

The purpose of the second weekend is to follow up on the problem-solving work begun the previous weekend and to move toward an action plan for dealing with new problems as they arise. It gives an opportunity to come back for more learning and support after having lived for a week "on your own" in the backhome environment. Some couples come back elated with feelings of success. Others return reluctantly — visibly unsure of "whether it's worth the struggle." Since weekend #1 has made them especially conscious of themselves as a couple, they will now be more sensitive to "how they're doing" and more sensitive to feelings of both success and failure.

The design of the second weekend aims at giving couples the opportunity to practice awareness and problem-solving skills in the areas where they most need it — whether their issues relate to romance, power, stability, commitment, co-creation or something else. Most of the time is spent in a 3-part sequence:

(1) a structured activity (such as those listed in Chapter 8) focusing on a particular problem area; followed by

(2) one or more couples working with me in the large group (as in the Sunday afternoon session on the first weekend); followed by

(3) work in quartets to go more deeply into the issues raised in the first two parts of the sequence.

Since (1) and (2) have essentially been described with reference to the first weekend, I'll elaborate only on (3).

By Saturday afternoon, the quartet structure is becoming the major learning vehicle for the workshop. Now, in addition to simply listening and "playing back the tape," consultants take more initiative in facilitating the inner dialogue/empty chair process I have been demonstrating in the large group sessions (as described in the case of Phil and Carolyn). Consultants are instructed to simply witness the other couple's communication as long as real contact is occurring; but if an impasse develops, some intervention by the consultants is called for. The form of that intervention is simply to ask each in turn to "put your partner in the empty chair and continue the dialogue, playing the roles of both yourself and him or her." Since all have witnessed this structure several times in my large group demonstrations, very little facilitation is actually needed.

What develops out of this process may be a "re-owning of projections," as in Phil and Carolyn's example. Or it could be getting clearer within oneself how one feels toward one's partner; expressing some old unfinished business; realizing that one is talking neither to one's partner nor to one's true inner self, but rather to some introjected parental or symbolic figure; or any one of a number of other surprises. The consultant pair simply keeps the inner dialogue going until some new awareness emerges to break the impasse or until the person working feels a new acceptance of responsibility for his or her predicament. Then, the couple goes back to dialoging face to face with each other, in order to integrate this developing self-awareness into their relationship.

Growth or development is seen here as a process which naturally accompanies such increased self-awareness. There is *no end state to be attained* but rather a continually-becoming-more-aware *process to be lived.*

B. *Action-planning*

The action-planning phase of the workshop deals more with the question "how can we continue to renew our relationship?" than with concern over "how to reach stability or commitment or maturity." Since life is seen as a process to be *lived* and *enjoyed* (when things are going well) and *learned from* (when they aren't), our action goals are more process-goals than product-goals. The focus on developmental stages is simply a structure for guiding the problem-solving process. It gives people a way of conceptualizing what they're doing, thus helping to make sense out of the way in which past, present, and future merge in the *now* of a particular experience.

The aim of the action-planning phase is to discover or create a problem-solving process that works. It may incorporate some of the structured activities introduced in the workshop. It might also include continuing to meet in quartets after the workshop, as an on-going support and consultation network. Or it could be something new that the couples choose to design for themselves based on their learnings during the weekend.

To design a plan for action, couples meet together to review learnings, insights, and feelings experienced during the workshop.

1. Self- Other- and Relationship-Assessment

Individually and together, they review their answers to the following questions, first answered during the self-assessment period at the beginning of the workshop.

   a. When do I feel most fulfilled in this relationship?

   b. When do I feel least fulfilled in this relationship?

   c. What do I do and what does my partner do which contributes to such fulfillment and lack of fulfillment?

   d. What would need to change in my own and in my partner's behavior to transform the least fulfilling situations into more fulfilling ones?

e. What can I learn from this relationship even if nothing changes?

2. Polarity Consciousness

Then, the partners together arrive at answers to the following questions:

a. What polarities or paradoxes are we facing in our life together? (e.g. closeness-distance, stability-change, masculine-feminine, play-work, power-vulnerability, excitement-calmness) See last half of Chapter 4 and Table II for a fuller explication of the notions of paradox and polarity.

c. Describe some behaviors and concrete situations which exemplify the mid-ranges of each continuum.

d. Which of these behaviors come most easily to us? Which are more difficult?

3. Creating a new structure

Now, the couple looks at what they want in the future:

a. How would we like to change our behavior to bring us to a different point on the continuum? What will we have to give up if we do this? What will we gain? Is it worth the cost?

b. If we are unsure about our commitment to a change, is there a way we can experiment with some new behaviors or situational structures (rules, games) without making an irreversible decision? Can we commit ourselves to this new structure as an experiment?

c. How will we know whether or not the new structure is meeting our needs? What will we feel like? What will be different or better about our lives?

d. How will we know when the new structure has outlived its usefulness? How will we know when it's time to create another new structure for ourselves?

Arriving at clear objectives and plans based on valid and current information about both partners' wants is a self- and relationship-renewal process that can be used over and over. People and relationships change over time, and the only way to maintain some sense of continuity in a changing environment without becoming stagnant is to adopt some sort of process for continued development. I call such processes "liberating structures" since they blend the freedom to grow and change (liberation) with the need for stability (structure).

The continual creation of more liberating structures simply involves the willingness to experiment with something new and to evaluate whether or not this meets our needs better than the old structure. If it does, we keep it. If it doesn't we try something else. With this attitude, every problem encountered by a couple is seen as an opportunity to learn more about what does and doesn't satisfy us, and about our range of options for creating higher consciousness and meaning in our lives and in those of others around us.

4. Quartet Work

A good way to insure that plans will be acted upon is to make a "public commitment" to follow through. This is done in quartets both because a relationship of trust and support has already been established here, and in order to encourage quartets to meet together after the workshop. It is a way of giving the groups a reason for being in one's life beyond the workshop. Such an ongoing relationship must be voluntary, of course.

My charge to the quartets is to review each others' action plans, with special attention to being *very specific* about *who* will do *what*, *when* and *how*. Also, it may be a good idea to agree upon the **probable** *consequences* of not following through on one's plans. When carried on in the spirit of shared growth, this "monitoring function" of the quartets can be an occasion for enjoyment as well as learning.

5. Large Group Closing

The final session occurs in two parts:

A. Milling

Here everyone has a chance to mill around and speak to anyone they wish to contact individually for the purpose of saying goodbye, giving feedback, clearing up unfinished business, or planning future meetings. This activity allows participants to leave the workshop feeling a sense of closure.

B. Sharing in the Large Group

When we reassemble for our last large group session, I invite "testimonials" from participants concerning either learnings during the workshop or plans for the weeks ahead. This is another opportunity for couples to publicly commit themselves to continued self-realization.

While the workshop generally ends on a note of positive expectations, I'm always careful to underscore the potential for disappointment inherent in great expectations. The ability to forgive and begin again, I maintain, is the basic foundation for any lasting relationship.

Thus, the workshop ends with couples appreciating both their courage to risk and explore, and their fallibility — with a balanced sense of excitement about new possibilities and confidence that we can continue to learn from our experience.